The Industrial Revolution: A Very Short Introduction

VERY SHORT INTRODUCTIONS are for anyone wanting a stimulating and accessible way into a new subject. They are written by experts, and have been translated into more than 45 different languages.

The series began in 1995, and now covers a wide variety of topics in every discipline. The VSI library now contains over 500 volumes—a Very Short Introduction to everything from Psychology and Philosophy of Science to American History and Relativity—and continues to grow in every subject area.

Very Short Introductions available now:

ACCOUNTING Christopher Nobes
ADOLESCENCE Peter K. Smith
ADVERTISING Winston Fletcher
AFRICAN AMERICAN RELIGION
    Eddie S. Glaude Jr
AFRICAN HISTORY John Parker and
    Richard Rathbone
AFRICAN RELIGIONS
    Jacob K. Olupona
AGEING Nancy A. Pachana
AGNOSTICISM Robin Le Poidevin
AGRICULTURE Paul Brassley and
    Richard Soffe
ALEXANDER THE GREAT
    Hugh Bowden
ALGEBRA Peter M. Higgins
AMERICAN HISTORY Paul S. Boyer
AMERICAN IMMIGRATION
    David A. Gerber
AMERICAN LEGAL HISTORY
    G. Edward White
AMERICAN POLITICAL HISTORY
    Donald Critchlow
AMERICAN POLITICAL PARTIES
    AND ELECTIONS L. Sandy Maisel
AMERICAN POLITICS
    Richard M. Valelly
THE AMERICAN PRESIDENCY
    Charles O. Jones
THE AMERICAN REVOLUTION
    Robert J. Allison
AMERICAN SLAVERY
    Heather Andrea Williams
THE AMERICAN WEST Stephen Aron

AMERICAN WOMEN'S HISTORY
    Susan Ware
ANAESTHESIA Aidan O'Donnell
ANARCHISM Colin Ward
ANCIENT ASSYRIA Karen Radner
ANCIENT EGYPT Ian Shaw
ANCIENT EGYPTIAN ART AND
    ARCHITECTURE Christina Riggs
ANCIENT GREECE Paul Cartledge
THE ANCIENT NEAR EAST
    Amanda H. Podany
ANCIENT PHILOSOPHY Julia Annas
ANCIENT WARFARE
    Harry Sidebottom
ANGELS David Albert Jones
ANGLICANISM Mark Chapman
THE ANGLO-SAXON AGE John Blair
THE ANIMAL KINGDOM
    Peter Holland
ANIMAL RIGHTS David DeGrazia
THE ANTARCTIC Klaus Dodds
ANTISEMITISM Steven Beller
ANXIETY Daniel Freeman and
    Jason Freeman
THE APOCRYPHAL GOSPELS
    Paul Foster
ARCHAEOLOGY Paul Bahn
ARCHITECTURE Andrew Ballantyne
ARISTOCRACY William Doyle
ARISTOTLE Jonathan Barnes
ART HISTORY Dana Arnold
ART THEORY Cynthia Freeland
ASIAN AMERICAN HISTORY
    Madeline Y. Hsu

ASTROBIOLOGY David C. Catling
ASTROPHYSICS James Binney
ATHEISM Julian Baggini
AUGUSTINE Henry Chadwick
AUSTRALIA Kenneth Morgan
AUTISM Uta Frith
THE AVANT GARDE David Cottington
THE AZTECS David Carrasco
BABYLONIA Trevor Bryce
BACTERIA Sebastian G. B. Amyes
BANKING John Goddard and
    John O. S. Wilson
BARTHES Jonathan Culler
THE BEATS David Sterritt
BEAUTY Roger Scruton
BEHAVIOURAL ECONOMICS
    Michelle Baddeley
BESTSELLERS John Sutherland
THE BIBLE John Riches
BIBLICAL ARCHAEOLOGY Eric H. Cline
BIOGRAPHY Hermione Lee
BLACK HOLES Katherine Blundell
BLOOD Chris Cooper
THE BLUES Elijah Wald
THE BODY Chris Shilling
THE BOOK OF MORMON
    Terryl Givens
BORDERS Alexander C. Diener and
    Joshua Hagen
THE BRAIN Michael O'Shea
THE BRICS Andrew F. Cooper
THE BRITISH CONSTITUTION
    Martin Loughlin
THE BRITISH EMPIRE Ashley Jackson
BRITISH POLITICS Anthony Wright
BUDDHA Michael Carrithers
BUDDHISM Damien Keown
BUDDHIST ETHICS Damien Keown
BYZANTIUM Peter Sarris
CALVINISM Jon Balserak
CANCER Nicholas James
CAPITALISM James Fulcher
CATHOLICISM Gerald O'Collins
CAUSATION Stephen Mumford and
    Rani Lill Anjum
THE CELL Terence Allen and
    Graham Cowling
THE CELTS Barry Cunliffe
CHAOS Leonard Smith
CHEMISTRY Peter Atkins

CHILD PSYCHOLOGY Usha Goswami
CHILDREN'S LITERATURE
    Kimberley Reynolds
CHINESE LITERATURE Sabina Knight
CHOICE THEORY Michael Allingham
CHRISTIAN ART Beth Williamson
CHRISTIAN ETHICS D. Stephen Long
CHRISTIANITY Linda Woodhead
CITIZENSHIP Richard Bellamy
CIVIL ENGINEERING David Muir Wood
CLASSICAL LITERATURE William Allan
CLASSICAL MYTHOLOGY
    Helen Morales
CLASSICS Mary Beard and
    John Henderson
CLAUSEWITZ Michael Howard
CLIMATE Mark Maslin
CLIMATE CHANGE Mark Maslin
COGNITIVE NEUROSCIENCE
    Richard Passingham
THE COLD WAR Robert McMahon
COLONIAL AMERICA Alan Taylor
COLONIAL LATIN AMERICAN
    LITERATURE Rolena Adorno
COMBINATORICS Robin Wilson
COMEDY Matthew Bevis
COMMUNISM Leslie Holmes
COMPLEXITY John H. Holland
THE COMPUTER Darrel Ince
COMPUTER SCIENCE
    Subrata Dasgupta
CONFUCIANISM Daniel K. Gardner
THE CONQUISTADORS
    Matthew Restall and
    Felipe Fernández-Armesto
CONSCIENCE Paul Strohm
CONSCIOUSNESS Susan Blackmore
CONTEMPORARY ART
    Julian Stallabrass
CONTEMPORARY FICTION
    Robert Eaglestone
CONTINENTAL PHILOSOPHY
    Simon Critchley
COPERNICUS Owen Gingerich
CORAL REEFS Charles Sheppard
CORPORATE SOCIAL
    RESPONSIBILITY Jeremy Moon
CORRUPTION Leslie Holmes
COSMOLOGY Peter Coles
CRIME FICTION Richard Bradford

CRIMINAL JUSTICE Julian V. Roberts
CRITICAL THEORY
  Stephen Eric Bronner
THE CRUSADES Christopher Tyerman
CRYPTOGRAPHY Fred Piper and
  Sean Murphy
CRYSTALLOGRAPHY A. M. Glazer
THE CULTURAL REVOLUTION
  Richard Curt Kraus
DADA AND SURREALISM
  David Hopkins
DANTE Peter Hainsworth and
  David Robey
DARWIN Jonathan Howard
THE DEAD SEA SCROLLS Timothy Lim
DECOLONIZATION Dane Kennedy
DEMOCRACY Bernard Crick
DEPRESSION Jan Scott and
  Mary Jane Tacchi
DERRIDA Simon Glendinning
DESCARTES Tom Sorell
DESERTS Nick Middleton
DESIGN John Heskett
DEVELOPMENTAL BIOLOGY
  Lewis Wolpert
THE DEVIL Darren Oldridge
DIASPORA Kevin Kenny
DICTIONARIES Lynda Mugglestone
DINOSAURS David Norman
DIPLOMACY Joseph M. Siracusa
DOCUMENTARY FILM
  Patricia Aufderheide
DREAMING J. Allan Hobson
DRUGS Les Iversen
DRUIDS Barry Cunliffe
EARLY MUSIC Thomas Forrest Kelly
THE EARTH Martin Redfern
EARTH SYSTEM SCIENCE Tim Lenton
ECONOMICS Partha Dasgupta
EDUCATION Gary Thomas
EGYPTIAN MYTH Geraldine Pinch
EIGHTEENTH-CENTURY BRITAIN
  Paul Langford
THE ELEMENTS Philip Ball
EMOTION Dylan Evans
EMPIRE Stephen Howe
ENGELS Terrell Carver
ENGINEERING David Blockley
ENGLISH LITERATURE Jonathan Bate
THE ENLIGHTENMENT
  John Robertson

ENTREPRENEURSHIP Paul Westhead
  and Mike Wright
ENVIRONMENTAL ECONOMICS
  Stephen Smith
ENVIRONMENTAL POLITICS
  Andrew Dobson
EPICUREANISM Catherine Wilson
EPIDEMIOLOGY Rodolfo Saracci
ETHICS Simon Blackburn
ETHNOMUSICOLOGY Timothy Rice
THE ETRUSCANS Christopher Smith
EUGENICS Philippa Levine
THE EUROPEAN UNION John Pinder
  and Simon Usherwood
EVOLUTION Brian and
  Deborah Charlesworth
EXISTENTIALISM Thomas Flynn
EXPLORATION Stewart A. Weaver
THE EYE Michael Land
FAMILY LAW Jonathan Herring
FASCISM Kevin Passmore
FASHION Rebecca Arnold
FEMINISM Margaret Walters
FILM Michael Wood
FILM MUSIC Kathryn Kalinak
THE FIRST WORLD WAR
  Michael Howard
FOLK MUSIC Mark Slobin
FOOD John Krebs
FORENSIC PSYCHOLOGY David Canter
FORENSIC SCIENCE Jim Fraser
FORESTS Jaboury Ghazoul
FOSSILS Keith Thomson
FOUCAULT Gary Gutting
THE FOUNDING FATHERS
  R. B. Bernstein
FRACTALS Kenneth Falconer
FREE SPEECH Nigel Warburton
FREE WILL Thomas Pink
FRENCH LITERATURE John D. Lyons
THE FRENCH REVOLUTION
  William Doyle
FREUD Anthony Storr
FUNDAMENTALISM Malise Ruthven
FUNGI Nicholas P. Money
GALAXIES John Gribbin
GALILEO Stillman Drake
GAME THEORY Ken Binmore
GANDHI Bhikhu Parekh
GENES Jonathan Slack
GENIUS Andrew Robinson

GEOGRAPHY John Matthews
  and David Herbert
GEOPOLITICS Klaus Dodds
GERMAN LITERATURE Nicholas Boyle
GERMAN PHILOSOPHY
  Andrew Bowie
GLOBAL CATASTROPHES Bill McGuire
GLOBAL ECONOMIC HISTORY
  Robert C. Allen
GLOBALIZATION Manfred Steger
GOD John Bowker
GOETHE Ritchie Robertson
THE GOTHIC Nick Groom
GOVERNANCE Mark Bevir
THE GREAT DEPRESSION AND
  THE NEW DEAL Eric Rauchway
HABERMAS James Gordon Finlayson
HAPPINESS Daniel M. Haybron
THE HARLEM RENAISSANCE
  Cheryl A. Wall
THE HEBREW BIBLE AS LITERATURE
  Tod Linafelt
HEGEL Peter Singer
HEIDEGGER Michael Inwood
HERMENEUTICS Jens Zimmermann
HERODOTUS Jennifer T. Roberts
HIEROGLYPHS Penelope Wilson
HINDUISM Kim Knott
HISTORY John H. Arnold
THE HISTORY of ASTRONOMY
  Michael Hoskin
THE HISTORY OF CHEMISTRY
  William H. Brock
THE HISTORY OF LIFE Michael Benton
THE HISTORY OF MATHEMATICS
  Jacqueline Stedall
THE HISTORY OF MEDICINE
  William Bynum
THE HISTORY OF TIME
  Leofranc Holford-Strevens
HIV AND AIDS Alan Whiteside
HOBBES Richard Tuck
HOLLYWOOD Peter Decherney
HOME Michael Allen Fox
HORMONES Martin Luck
HUMAN ANATOMY Leslie Klenerman
HUMAN EVOLUTION Bernard Wood
HUMAN RIGHTS Andrew Clapham
HUMANISM Stephen Law
HUME A. J. Ayer
HUMOUR Noël Carroll

THE ICE AGE Jamie Woodward
IDEOLOGY Michael Freeden
INDIAN CINEMA Ashish Rajadhyaksha
INDIAN PHILOSOPHY Sue Hamilton
THE INDUSTRIAL REVOLUTION
  Robert C. Allen
INFECTIOUS DISEASE Marta L. Wayne
  and Benjamin M. Bolker
INFORMATION Luciano Floridi
INNOVATION Mark Dodgson
  and David Gann
INTELLIGENCE Ian J. Deary
INTELLECTUAL PROPERTY
  Siva Vaidhyanathan
INTERNATIONAL LAW Vaughan Lowe
INTERNATIONAL MIGRATION
  Khalid Koser
INTERNATIONAL RELATIONS
  Paul Wilkinson
INTERNATIONAL SECURITY
  Christopher S. Browning
IRAN Ali M. Ansari
ISLAM Malise Ruthven
ISLAMIC HISTORY Adam Silverstein
ISOTOPES Rob Ellam
ITALIAN LITERATURE
  Peter Hainsworth and David Robey
JESUS Richard Bauckham
JOURNALISM Ian Hargreaves
JUDAISM Norman Solomon
JUNG Anthony Stevens
KABBALAH Joseph Dan
KAFKA Ritchie Robertson
KANT Roger Scruton
KEYNES Robert Skidelsky
KIERKEGAARD Patrick Gardiner
KNOWLEDGE Jennifer Nagel
THE KORAN Michael Cook
LANDSCAPE ARCHITECTURE
  Ian H. Thompson
LANDSCAPES AND
  GEOMORPHOLOGY
  Andrew Goudie and Heather Viles
LANGUAGES Stephen R. Anderson
LATE ANTIQUITY Gillian Clark
LAW Raymond Wacks
THE LAWS OF THERMODYNAMICS
  Peter Atkins
LEADERSHIP Keith Grint
LEARNING Mark Haselgrove
LEIBNIZ Maria Rosa Antognazza

LIBERALISM Michael Freeden
LIGHT Ian Walmsley
LINCOLN Allen C. Guelzo
LINGUISTICS Peter Matthews
LITERARY THEORY Jonathan Culler
LOCKE John Dunn
LOGIC Graham Priest
LOVE Ronald de Sousa
MACHIAVELLI Quentin Skinner
MADNESS Andrew Scull
MAGIC Owen Davies
MAGNA CARTA Nicholas Vincent
MAGNETISM Stephen Blundell
MALTHUS Donald Winch
MANAGEMENT John Hendry
MAO Delia Davin
MARINE BIOLOGY Philip V. Mladenov
THE MARQUIS DE SADE John Phillips
MARTIN LUTHER Scott H. Hendrix
MARTYRDOM Jolyon Mitchell
MARX Peter Singer
MATERIALS Christopher Hall
MATHEMATICS Timothy Gowers
THE MEANING OF LIFE Terry Eagleton
MEASUREMENT David Hand
MEDICAL ETHICS Tony Hope
MEDICAL LAW Charles Foster
MEDIEVAL BRITAIN
    John Gillingham and Ralph A. Griffiths
MEDIEVAL LITERATURE
    Elaine Treharne
MEDIEVAL PHILOSOPHY
    John Marenbon
MEMORY Jonathan K. Foster
METAPHYSICS Stephen Mumford
THE MEXICAN REVOLUTION
    Alan Knight
MICHAEL FARADAY
    Frank A. J. L. James
MICROBIOLOGY Nicholas P. Money
MICROECONOMICS Avinash Dixit
MICROSCOPY Terence Allen
THE MIDDLE AGES Miri Rubin
MILITARY JUSTICE Eugene R. Fidell
MINERALS David Vaughan
MODERN ART David Cottington
MODERN CHINA Rana Mitter
MODERN DRAMA
    Kirsten E. Shepherd-Barr
MODERN FRANCE
    Vanessa R. Schwartz

MODERN IRELAND Senia Pašeta
MODERN ITALY Anna Cento Bull
MODERN JAPAN
    Christopher Goto-Jones
MODERN LATIN AMERICAN
    LITERATURE
    Roberto González Echevarría
MODERN WAR Richard English
MODERNISM Christopher Butler
MOLECULAR BIOLOGY Aysha Divan
    and Janice A. Royds
MOLECULES Philip Ball
THE MONGOLS Morris Rossabi
MOONS David A. Rothery
MORMONISM
    Richard Lyman Bushman
MOUNTAINS Martin F. Price
MUHAMMAD Jonathan A. C. Brown
MULTICULTURALISM Ali Rattansi
MUSIC Nicholas Cook
MYTH Robert A. Segal
THE NAPOLEONIC WARS
    Mike Rapport
NATIONALISM Steven Grosby
NELSON MANDELA Elleke Boehmer
NEOLIBERALISM Manfred Steger
    and Ravi Roy
NETWORKS Guido Caldarelli
    and Michele Catanzaro
THE NEW TESTAMENT
    Luke Timothy Johnson
THE NEW TESTAMENT AS
    LITERATURE Kyle Keefer
NEWTON Robert Iliffe
NIETZSCHE Michael Tanner
NINETEENTH-CENTURY BRITAIN
    Christopher Harvie and
    H. C. G. Matthew
THE NORMAN CONQUEST
    George Garnett
NORTH AMERICAN INDIANS
    Theda Perdue and Michael D. Green
NORTHERN IRELAND
    Marc Mulholland
NOTHING Frank Close
NUCLEAR PHYSICS Frank Close
NUCLEAR POWER Maxwell Irvine
NUCLEAR WEAPONS
    Joseph M. Siracusa
NUMBERS Peter M. Higgins
NUTRITION David A. Bender

OBJECTIVITY Stephen Gaukroger
THE OLD TESTAMENT
   Michael D. Coogan
THE ORCHESTRA D. Kern Holoman
ORGANIZATIONS Mary Jo Hatch
PANDEMICS Christian W. McMillen
PAGANISM Owen Davies
THE PALESTINIAN-ISRAELI
   CONFLICT Martin Bunton
PARTICLE PHYSICS Frank Close
PAUL E. P. Sanders
PEACE Oliver P. Richmond
PENTECOSTALISM William K. Kay
THE PERIODIC TABLE Eric R. Scerri
PHILOSOPHY Edward Craig
PHILOSOPHY IN THE ISLAMIC
   WORLD Peter Adamson
PHILOSOPHY OF LAW
   Raymond Wacks
PHILOSOPHY OF SCIENCE
   Samir Okasha
PHOTOGRAPHY Steve Edwards
PHYSICAL CHEMISTRY Peter Atkins
PILGRIMAGE Ian Reader
PLAGUE Paul Slack
PLANETS David A. Rothery
PLANTS Timothy Walker
PLATE TECTONICS Peter Molnar
PLATO Julia Annas
POLITICAL PHILOSOPHY
   David Miller
POLITICS Kenneth Minogue
POPULISM Cas Mudde and
   Cristóbal Rovira Kaltwasser
POSTCOLONIALISM Robert Young
POSTMODERNISM Christopher Butler
POSTSTRUCTURALISM
   Catherine Belsey
PREHISTORY Chris Gosden
PRESOCRATIC PHILOSOPHY
   Catherine Osborne
PRIVACY Raymond Wacks
PROBABILITY John Haigh
PROGRESSIVISM Walter Nugent
PROTESTANTISM Mark A. Noll
PSYCHIATRY Tom Burns
PSYCHOANALYSIS Daniel Pick
PSYCHOLOGY Gillian Butler and
   Freda McManus
PSYCHOTHERAPY Tom Burns and
   Eva Burns-Lundgren

PUBLIC ADMINISTRATION
   Stella Z. Theodoulou and Ravi K. Roy
PUBLIC HEALTH Virginia Berridge
PURITANISM Francis J. Bremer
THE QUAKERS Pink Dandelion
QUANTUM THEORY
   John Polkinghorne
RACISM Ali Rattansi
RADIOACTIVITY Claudio Tuniz
RASTAFARI Ennis B. Edmonds
THE REAGAN REVOLUTION Gil Troy
REALITY Jan Westerhoff
THE REFORMATION Peter Marshall
RELATIVITY Russell Stannard
RELIGION IN AMERICA Timothy Beal
THE RENAISSANCE Jerry Brotton
RENAISSANCE ART
   Geraldine A. Johnson
REVOLUTIONS Jack A. Goldstone
RHETORIC Richard Toye
RISK Baruch Fischhoff and John Kadvany
RITUAL Barry Stephenson
RIVERS Nick Middleton
ROBOTICS Alan Winfield
ROCKS Jan Zalasiewicz
ROMAN BRITAIN Peter Salway
THE ROMAN EMPIRE
   Christopher Kelly
THE ROMAN REPUBLIC
   David M. Gwynn
ROMANTICISM Michael Ferber
ROUSSEAU Robert Wokler
RUSSELL A. C. Grayling
RUSSIAN HISTORY Geoffrey Hosking
RUSSIAN LITERATURE Catriona Kelly
THE RUSSIAN REVOLUTION
   S. A. Smith
SAVANNAS Peter A. Furley
SCHIZOPHRENIA Chris Frith and
   Eve Johnstone
SCHOPENHAUER
   Christopher Janaway
SCIENCE AND RELIGION
   Thomas Dixon
SCIENCE FICTION David Seed
THE SCIENTIFIC REVOLUTION
   Lawrence M. Principe
SCOTLAND Rab Houston
SEXUALITY Véronique Mottier
SHAKESPEARE'S COMEDIES
   Bart van Es

SIKHISM Eleanor Nesbitt
THE SILK ROAD James A. Millward
SLANG Jonathon Green
SLEEP Steven W. Lockley and
    Russell G. Foster
SOCIAL AND CULTURAL
    ANTHROPOLOGY
    John Monaghan and Peter Just
SOCIAL PSYCHOLOGY Richard J. Crisp
SOCIAL WORK Sally Holland and
    Jonathan Scourfield
SOCIALISM Michael Newman
SOCIOLINGUISTICS John Edwards
SOCIOLOGY Steve Bruce
SOCRATES C. C. W. Taylor
SOUND Mike Goldsmith
THE SOVIET UNION Stephen Lovell
THE SPANISH CIVIL WAR
    Helen Graham
SPANISH LITERATURE Jo Labanyi
SPINOZA Roger Scruton
SPIRITUALITY Philip Sheldrake
SPORT Mike Cronin
STARS Andrew King
STATISTICS David J. Hand
STEM CELLS Jonathan Slack
STRUCTURAL ENGINEERING
    David Blockley
STUART BRITAIN John Morrill
SUPERCONDUCTIVITY
    Stephen Blundell
SYMMETRY Ian Stewart
TAXATION Stephen Smith
TEETH Peter S. Ungar
TELESCOPES Geoff Cottrell
TERRORISM Charles Townshend
THEATRE Marvin Carlson

THEOLOGY David F. Ford
THOMAS AQUINAS Fergus Kerr
THOUGHT Tim Bayne
TIBETAN BUDDHISM
    Matthew T. Kapstein
TOCQUEVILLE Harvey C. Mansfield
TRAGEDY Adrian Poole
TRANSLATION Matthew Reynolds
THE TROJAN WAR Eric H. Cline
TRUST Katherine Hawley
THE TUDORS John Guy
TWENTIETH-CENTURY BRITAIN
    Kenneth O. Morgan
THE UNITED NATIONS
    Jussi M. Hanhimäki
THE U.S. CONGRESS Donald A. Ritchie
THE U.S. SUPREME COURT
    Linda Greenhouse
UTOPIANISM Lyman Tower Sargent
THE VIKINGS Julian Richards
VIRUSES Dorothy H. Crawford
WAR AND TECHNOLOGY Alex Roland
WATER John Finney
WEATHER Storm Dunlop
THE WELFARE STATE David Garland
WILLIAM SHAKESPEARE
    Stanley Wells
WITCHCRAFT Malcolm Gaskill
WITTGENSTEIN A. C. Grayling
WORK Stephen Fineman
WORLD MUSIC Philip Bohlman
THE WORLD TRADE
    ORGANIZATION Amrita Narlikar
WORLD WAR II Gerhard L. Weinberg
WRITING AND SCRIPT
    Andrew Robinson
ZIONISM Michael Stanislawski

Available soon:

GRAVITY Timothy Clifton
VOLTAIRE Nicholas Cronk
MILITARY STRATEGY
    Antulio J. Echevarria

ANIMAL BEHAVIOUR
    Tristram D. Wyatt

For more information visit our website

www.oup.com/vsi/

Robert C. Allen

THE INDUSTRIAL REVOLUTION

A Very Short Introduction

OXFORD
UNIVERSITY PRESS

OXFORD

UNIVERSITY PRESS

Great Clarendon Street, Oxford, OX2 6DP,
United Kingdom

Oxford University Press is a department of the University of Oxford.
It furthers the University's objective of excellence in research, scholarship,
and education by publishing worldwide. Oxford is a registered trade mark of
Oxford University Press in the UK and in certain other countries

Published in the United States of America by Oxford University Press
198 Madison Avenue, New York, NY 10016, United States of America

British Library Cataloguing in Publication Data

Data available

Library of Congress Control Number: 2016952561

ISBN 978–0–19–870678–6

Printed and bound by
CPI Group (UK) Ltd, Croydon, CR0 4YY

Contents

Acknowledgements xiii

List of illustrations xv

1   Then and now 1

2   The pre-Industrial Revolution, 1500–1700 15

3   Why the Industrial Revolution was British 35

4   The condition of England 60

5   Reform and democracy 84

6   The spread of the Industrial Revolution abroad 106

References 129

Further reading 135

Publisher's acknowledgements 143

Index 144

Acknowledgements

I am grateful to Andrea Keegan of Oxford University Press, who has had the confidence—twice now!—to sign me up to write a VSI.

Much of Chapter 3 appeared originally as Robert C. Allen, 'Technology', in Roderick Floud, Jane Humphries, and Paul Johnson (eds), *Cambridge Economic History of Modern Britain*. Cambridge: Cambridge University Press, 2014: Vol. 1, pp. 292–320. I thank Cambridge University Press for permission to use this material.

I thank the following people for reading the manuscript and giving me their comments: Dianne Frank, Matthew Allen, Ligita Vicokyte, Stan Engerman, Patrick O'Brien, Petra Moser, Peter Temin, and the readers for OUP. I benefited greatly from their reactions. Remaining errors are, of course, my own.

Writing a book always takes more time than it is supposed to, and that time is stolen from weekends, evenings, and holidays. I am thankful for the understanding of my wife Dianne and my son Matthew when I missed planting trees, building walls, cycling across Europe, and visiting museums and stately homes. Dianne does bear some of the responsibility, however: when I was in a bookstore with Matthew marvelling at a display of Very Short

Introductions, it was Dianne who burst out: 'You could write one of those!' And so here we are.

Stan Engerman and Peter Temin are great scholars whose work has inspired me and taught me much. They have offered me advice and encouragement, friendship and support over my career, and I am immensely grateful for that. I am pleased to dedicate this book to them.

List of illustrations

1 Detail from *Proverbios flamencos* by Pieter Bruegel, the Elder **xviii**

Gemäldegalerie, Berlin. © World History Archive/age footstock

2 GDP per worker versus the average real wage **8**

Based on data series explained in Robert C. Allen, 'Engel's Pause: Technical Change, Capital Accumulation, and Inequality in the British Industrial Revolution', *Explorations in Economic History* 46 (2009): 418–35. The real GDP series discussed in the article has been replaced by the new real GDP series developed by Stephen Broadberry, Alexander Klein, Bas van Leeuwen, Bruce Campbell, and Mark Overton, *British Economic Growth, 1270–1870*. Cambridge: Cambridge University Press, 2015: 241–4

3 Early's point blankets **16**

Reproduced with permission of Oxfordshire Museums Service (OXCMS: 2004.134.66)

4 A south-east view of the city of Boston, *c*.1730 **23**

Yale Center for British Art, Paul Mellon Collection

5 Population and the real wage in England, 1300–1750 **27**

See Robert C. Allen, 'Poverty and Progress in Early Modern Europe', *Economic History Review* LVI (2003): 403–43

6 Wages relative to the cost of subsistence around the world **31**

Drawn with data underlying figure 6 on p. 19 in Robert C. Allen, 'The High Wage Economy and the Industrial Revolution: A Restatement', *The Economic History Review* 2015: 68: 1–22

7 Irish cottage with handloom weaver and spinner **38**

© Mary Evans Picture Library/ Alamy Stock Photo

8 Factory spinning **40**

Courtesy of the Library of Congress

9 Diagram of Newcomen steam engine **46**

From Black & Davis, *Practical Physics for Secondary Schools: Fundamental Principles and Applications to Daily Life* (Macmillan, 1913)/Wikimedia Commons

10 Plate decorated in willow pattern **56**

© Hanley Museum & Art Gallery, Staffordshire, UK/Bridgeman Images

11 Richard Arkwright and his water frame **68**

(a) © iStock.com/mashuk; (b) © Science Museum/Science & Society Picture Library—all rights reserved

12 Real wages in Lancashire **72**

Farm labourer and building labourer as explained in Robert C. Allen, 'The High Wage Economy and the Industrial Revolution: A Restatement', *The Economic History Review* 68 (2015): 8 and 19. Handloom weaver is a cotton weaver and earnings follow C.H. Feinstein, 'Wage-earnings in Great Britain during the Industrial Revolution', in Iain Begg and S.G.B. Henry (eds), *Applied Economics and Public Policy*. Cambridge: Cambridge University Press, 1998: 189; and G.H. Wood, 'The Statistics of Wages in the United Kingdom During the Nineteenth Century. Part XVIII and XIX: The Cotton Industry', *Journal of the Royal Statistical Society* 73: 425–33 and 598–9

13 Peterloo massacre **92**

Cartoon by George Cruikshank. Wikimedia Commons

14 Price of wheat, 1785–1875 **93**

England is the *London Gazette* price from Brian R. Mitchell and Phyllis Deane, *Abstract of British Historical Statistics*. Cambridge: Cambridge University Press, 1971: 488–9. The Amsterdam price is that of Frisian wheat from N.W. Posthumus, *Inquiry into the History of Prices in Holland*. Leiden: E.J. Brill, 1946: Vol. I, pp. 10–12

15 Detail of the Newport rising **103**

Mural by Kenneth Budd. © REX/Shutterstock

16 Percentage shares of world manufacturing output, 1750–2013 **107**

Paul Bairoch, 'International Industrialization Levels from 1750 to 1980', *Journal of European Economic History* 11 (1982): 269–333: and World Bank, *World Development Indicators*, various years

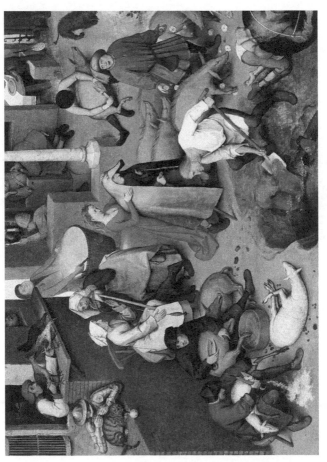

1. Detail from *Proverbios flamencos* by Pieter Bruegel, the Elder.

Chapter 1
Then and now

The question is: why don't we live in a Bruegel painting? Pieter Bruegel depicted everyday life in the small towns and villages of 16th-century Flanders (see Figure 1). Peasants drove horse drawn ploughs and carts. Townsmen worked in small shops with hand tools to weave cloth, slaughter pigs, and bake bread. Indeed, there was a good deal of emphasis on food, which bulked large in the economy.

Churches were prominent.

Entertainment revolved around village fetes.

It's all different today, of course. Hand tools are the preserve of the hobbyist.

Production is undertaken in large factories with machines and robots. Our homes are heated with electricity and gas: wood belongs in the fireplace and charcoal in the barbecue. We drive cars, fly planes, talk on mobiles. We live in great cities. Farmers make up only a few per cent of the population. The countryside is for walks where we 'reconnect' with nature.

It has taken centuries to get from then to now. The Industrial Revolution was a decisive juncture on that journey, and it occurred at the halfway point between Bruegel's era and today.

'Industrial Revolution' refers to the far reaching transformation of British society that occurred between the mid-18th and mid-19th centuries. The Revolution wears the two faces of Dr Jekyll and Mr Hyde. On the plus side, manufacturing technology was revolutionized as factories replaced handicraft methods. Productivity leaped up through the invention of machines to spin and weave cloth; the perfection of the steam engine so that it became a widely used source of power; the replacement of charcoal by coal in the smelting and refining of iron; and the construction of the first railways. Cheap coal displaced expensive renewable energy sources like wood, water, and wind. The continuous search for improved methods of production became normal business practice. Cities grew as people shifted from farming to industry and commerce. Productivity and national output have risen since the mid-18th century to produce an enviable prosperity in the West. This is the benevolent face of Dr Jekyll.

The Industrial Revolution also had a dark side, for it brought poverty as well as progress. This was Mr Hyde's malevolent face. Technical change threw many people out of work. Twelve-hour work days were normal in the new factories, and the remuneration was meagre. Workers' housing in the expanding cities was often squalid, and lacked effective sanitation and safe drinking water. The cities were polluted. The provision of education was limited. Some romantics rejected the new industrial order, and many writers explored its contradictions in the 'social problem novel'. Workers organized trade unions (although they were illegal) and protest movements to improve their conditions, while socialists plotted a better world order. Foreign observers were appalled—they wanted Britain's progress without its poverty. Why did the possibilities for a better life take so long to reach the working population?

The contradictions of the Industrial Revolution were intrinsic to its dynamics. The term itself is misleading in that it suggests a dramatic rupture with what came before—and that was certainly Toynbee's intention when he popularized the phrase in his *Lectures on the Industrial Revolution of the Eighteenth Century in England* (1884)—but historians now recognize that the Industrial Revolution was the culmination of two centuries of economic evolution. Following Columbus' voyage to the Caribbean in 1492, Europeans colonized the Americas, and the Atlantic economy boomed. England was particularly successful in this endeavour and established colonies along the east coast of the future USA and in the Caribbean. The Atlantic economy was a great market for English goods, and the handicraft sector grew in consequence—employing as much as a third of the workforce on the eve of the Industrial Revolution. This great increase in employment led to an agricultural revolution that fed the manufacturing population; an energy revolution as coal was exploited to heat the growing cities; and to wage levels that exceeded those in most other countries. High wages and cheap energy made it profitable to invent techniques that increased the use of capital and energy relative to labour—the power-driven machinery that raised productivity. These techniques were not profitable to use in France, Egypt, or India, so they were invented in Britain rather than elsewhere. This is why the Industrial Revolution was British.

The economy of the Industrial Revolution was unstable, however. As the machines were invented, they out-competed the handicraft sector whose large size had been responsible for the high wages that made labour-saving machines profitable in the first place. The adoption of machinery led to massive technological unemployment in one handicraft trade after another. The growth of the handicraft sector in the 17th and 18th centuries, thus, contained the seeds of its own destruction. The genius of capitalism consists as much in destroying the old production systems as it does in creating the new. The process is one that Schumpeter described as a 'perennial gale of creative destruction'. The gale blew strongly in the

Industrial Revolution producing poverty at the same time as it brought progress.

There were great gainers as well as great losers in the Industrial Revolution, and their aspirations and predicaments influenced social and political life generally. Most agricultural land was owned by perhaps 15,000 families, and members of this group dominated parliament and held most of the high political offices throughout the Industrial Revolution.

While the landowners claimed to act in the national interest, they often advanced their own at the expense of other groups—a notable example being the Corn Laws of 1815, which aimed to keep the price of wheat high in Britain by excluding cheap imported grain. Mass mobilization to extend the franchise and increase the representation of cities in parliament led to the Reform Act of 1832, which gave the vote to many in the middle class but not to the workers of the country. The Chartist movement in the 1830s and 1840s sought universal male suffrage, but these petitions were always rejected. The upper classes regarded democracy as a threat to their property and power so long as wages were stagnant and poverty was a source of discontent. It was only in the mid-19th century that machine production finally liquidated the hand trades. After that, wages started to rise as high productivity jobs were created faster than low productivity jobs were destroyed. The Industrial Revolution was finished, and, in 1867, the upper strata of the working class at last got the vote.

Reinforcing revolutions

One reason that the Industrial Revolution led to a continuous process of economic growth is that it involved a set of revolutions that reinforced each other. Some of these revolutions, in fact, started before the Industrial Revolution—therefore, the Industrial Revolution was the result of economic change as well as the cause of it.

Technological change is the motor that powers economic growth, and a *technological revolution* was at the heart of the Industrial Revolution. A schoolboy famously wrote: 'About 1760 a wave of gadgets swept over England.' The most celebrated gadgets were in the iron and cotton industries, and in power generation. Abraham Darby's successful smelting of pig iron with coke rather than charcoal, the traditional fuel, in 1709 initiated the changes in the iron industry. Huntsman revolutionized the production of steel with the crucible process in the 1740s; and Henry Cort did the same for wrought iron manufacture with the puddling and rolling processes in the 1780s. Cotton had always been spun by hand on wheels or with a distaff and spindle until James Hargreaves invented the spinning jenny in the 1760s; Richard Arkwright, the water frame in the 1770s; and Samuel Crompton, the mule ten years later.

Factory spinning was soon followed by the invention of power weaving by Edmund Cartwright around 1785, which took decades to perfect. Finally, power technology was shifted from traditional or organic sources (e.g. wood and charcoal, wind, water, and animals) to coal, with the invention of the steam engine by Thomas Newcomen in the early 1700s and its improvement by James Watt in the 1760s. These technologies were further perfected over the next century and a half, and breakthroughs were extended to other sectors like transportation, with the invention of the railway in the 1830s and the steamship. By the mid-19th century, mechanization was spreading across most of British industry. The continual revolutionizing of the mode of production and transportation is the greatest legacy of the Industrial Revolution.

A *demographic revolution* accompanied the technological changes. The population of Great Britain was constant at about 6.5 million between 1650 and 1750 after which it started to grow, reaching 10.5 million in 1800; 20.8 in 1850; 37 in 1900; and 50 million in 1950. Since then the rate of natural increase has been very low. The relationship between population growth and economic variables like industrialization, incomes, urbanization, and education has been the subject of research and debate since Malthus' seminal *Essay on the Principle of Population* (1798).

An *urban revolution* also occurred, but it started before the Industrial Revolution. In 1500 only 7 per cent of the English population lived in towns and cities of 5,000 people or more. By 1750 that fraction increased to 23 per cent—and it kept growing as the population expanded, reaching 50 per cent in 1850; and 75 per cent in 1910. London grew from small beginnings to become the largest city in Europe. The capital's population increased from 50,000 in 1500 to 200,000 in 1600; to 500,000 in 1700; and, finally, to one million in 1800.

An *agricultural revolution* was needed to feed the rapidly growing cities, and this began in the 17th century as grain yields rose, cows and sheep gave more milk and wool, and animals were reared to greater weights. The improvements were due to better seed selection, improved soil preparation (in part due to better equipment), selective breeding, and new crop rotations including fodder crops like turnips and clover. At the same time as farming practice was getting better, the common fields and pastures were being enclosed and small family farms were being combined into large 'capital' farms operated with hired labour. A long-standing view was that the enclosures and large farms were responsible for the improvements in practice and productivity, but that claim has been repeatedly called into question. Farm output continued to expand during the Industrial Revolution, but Britain became more and more dependent on imported food, as rising demand outstripped domestic supply.

Rising imports highlights another feature of Britain's transformation—a *commercial revolution*. Exports and imports became increasingly important relative to national income. This development also began early—by the end of the 16th century. In the 17th century, England exported increasing volumes of wool textiles, iron goods, and other manufactured items, while it imported ever more spices, sugar, tobacco, and tropical produce.

Once the Industrial Revolution got underway, exports of manufactured goods soared, while Britain imported raw cotton to spin into yarn and food to feed the growing workforce.

Transportation revolutions underpinned the growth in trade. In the 17th and 18th centuries, better sailing vessels cut ocean freight rates. In the 18th century, inland shipping costs fell as a canal system was built and roads were improved. Travel times were cut as vehicles went faster. After 1830, the railway further reduced overland transport costs, and steam ships eventually did the same for the seas. A world economy arose, and globalization promoted the industrialization of Britain, as it de-industrialized the Third World.

Economic growth required the construction of cities, factories, and transportation facilities, and the growth in commerce required an expansion of trade credit. These needs were met through a *financial revolution*. In the late 17th century, legal changes created the modern mortgage, so that land could be used as security to raise long term loans. English agricultural estates were mortgaged and the proceeds paid for the construction of cities. The public finances were reordered in the 1690s with the establishment of the Bank of England and the refunding of the national debt. Private banks developed in London that mainly financed international trade. The manufacturing firms of the Industrial Revolution started as small partnerships, and their factories were financed with the funds of the proprietors. As businesses came to outlive their owners, the corporate form of organization was permitted in manufacturing in the middle of the 19th century.

The macro picture

The upshot of these interlocking revolutions was a long run increase in GDP (gross domestic product = total output = the total income of Britain). In the last half century, there has been a concerted effort by economists and historians to measure this increase as well as the increases in the factors of production (land, labour, and capital) that were associated with it. Figure 2 shows real GDP per worker from 1770 to 1910. Output per worker doubled between 1770 and 1850, as GDP grew at just under 2 per cent per year. That is not much compared to recent growth miracles where GDP has leaped up as much as 10 per cent per annum, but progress is always slower for the leading economy that is pushing the world technology frontier forward than it is for a late developer that can copy the high productivity technology used in the advanced economies. This was particularly true for the first industrializer.

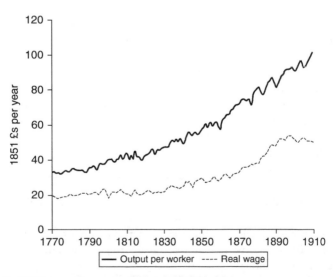

2. **GDP per worker versus the average real wage.**

Analysis of the GDP data shows that one reason that GDP per worker grew during the Industrial Revolution was capital accumulation: British workers had more machinery to work with at the end of the period than at the beginning. However, capital accumulation made only a small contribution to the growth in labour productivity. The biggest source of growth was technical progress—that is, the machinery and the organization of production were more efficient in the middle of the 19th century than they had been a century earlier.

Why was that? One approach has been to parcel out the growth in aggregate productivity to the various industries and sectors of the economy. Was the Industrial Revolution a uniform advance on all fronts or was progress confined to a few revolutionized industries? This is a precarious exercise given the poor quality of the data, but progress looks far from uniform. Between 1780 and 1860, the 'revolutionized' industries (principally textiles) accounted for 31 per cent of the growth in productivity; transport improvements (canals and ocean shipping) accounted for 18 per cent; and agriculture (perhaps surprisingly since this was an *industrial* revolution), for 29 per cent. That leaves only 15 per cent to be explained by advances in the rest of the economy. Many industries realized no productivity growth including those making flour, bread, beer, naval ships of the line, coal mining, and wood products like lath and wainscot. Others such as those making iron, shoes, stockings, paper, glass, nails, and steam and water power achieved substantial productivity growth.

Candle making is not usually given any attention in accounts of the Industrial Revolution, but it was, in fact, revolutionized. Productivity was static until the Napoleonic Wars, and then it doubled in a generation, growing at 2 per cent per year, which was even faster than productivity growth in cotton textiles. The production process in the 1840s was very different from the hand processes of earlier centuries. Candles were produced in moulds arranged in huge racks controlled by a single operator. Even the process of making dipped candles had become highly mechanized, so that a worker could produce great volumes. The mechanization of production raised productivity in candles as it did in cotton.

Gainers and losers

The Industrial Revolution led to a doubling of income per head in Britain between 1770 and 1870. Not everyone, however, shared in that advance. A big divide was between workers, on the one hand, and the middle and upper classes on the other. The division is highlighted in Figure 2, which plots the average real wage as well as real output per worker. While the latter doubled during the century of the Industrial Revolution, the former only increased by 50 per cent. Moreover, the rise in the real wage occurred at the end of the period. From 1770 to 1830 there was no discernible rise in the average real wage, and only a 5 per cent increase in the 1830s. It was only after about 1840 that the average worker began to participate in the progress of the Industrial Revolution.

Moreover, when we examine this question more closely in Chapter 4, we will see that the average real wage obscures as much as it reveals. Some workers experienced rising real incomes, while others, particularly those in the handicraft trades that were the basis of prosperity in the 18th century, had falling incomes as they faced competition from mechanized production. Poverty was the companion of prosperity.

Explaining the Industrial Revolution

Why did the Industrial Revolution happen in Britain rather than in France, the Netherlands, India, or China? There are many long-standing explanations that highlight background factors that played a part.

One influential theory attributes the Industrial Revolution to the rise of capitalism. According to Karl Marx, who stressed this explanation, capitalism was the only economic system in which incentives led to economic growth. In previous systems, redistributing income, rather than creating new income, was the surest way for people to improve their standard of living. Marx conceived of capitalism as a system with many competitive firms. Each firm had to increase its productivity or it would be driven out of business by competitors who would do so. The result was a high rate of capital accumulation and technological change. The secret to explaining growth was, therefore, explaining the rise of capitalism. Marx thought two channels were important. The first was the reorganization of rural society, so that feudal lords and peasant farmers operating in the open fields were replaced by landless labourers and large-scale 'capital' farms. While rural society did evolve in this way, it turns out that capitalist agriculture was not much more productive than the peasant agriculture which it replaced. On the other hand, 'the historical process of divorcing the producer from the means of production', that is, depriving the peasants of land, implements, and livestock so they had to become employees in order to survive, may have increased their readiness to take up handicraft production and migrate to cities to find work.

Marx also—and in this he has been joined by many other thinkers—stressed the importance of globalization in transforming the English economy. Inter-continental maritime trade increased gradually after the voyages of discovery of Columbus and Vasco da Gama at the end of the 15th century. Permanent settlements and colonies soon followed.

Europe's overseas expansion was accomplished by states competing for hegemony, and each used imperialism and trade policy to expand its wealth at the expense of its competitors (as well as the indigenous populations). Countries aimed to secure as much as possible of their colonies' trade for their own nationals through 'mercantilist' policies that excluded foreigners. When tariffs failed, war was an acceptable alternative. In this world, a country could succeed only through aggressive imperialism, and England proved to have one of the most growth promoting empires in Europe.

Slavery was a central feature of the global economy. Sugar, tobacco, and cotton were grown in the Caribbean and USA on plantations operated by slaves. These trades were substantial and lucrative, and the raw cotton imported by Britain from the USA after 1800 was the essential raw material of the Industrial Revolution. Many believe that the slave system was the foundation of the Industrial Revolution, and, in particular, that profits from slavery financed the accumulation of capital in Britain. But while there were case-by-case connections, profits from slavery in total were not substantial enough to explain the rise in investment that took place during the Industrial Revolution.

England's political and legal systems have been invoked by thinkers since Adam Smith as the key to explaining the Industrial Revolution. After the Norman Conquest in 1066, England had the most centralized feudal system in Europe. The nobles had considerable power both in parliament and on the battlefield, and they forced King John, for instance, to grant the Magna Carta in 1215. Disputes between Crown and Parliament in the 17th century resulted in the Civil War between the two, the execution of Charles I in 1649, Oliver Cromwell's commonwealth, and eventually the restoration of Charles II in 1660.

Parliamentary supremacy was definitively secured with the Glorious Revolution of 1688, when James II fled the country, and parliament gave the Crown to William and Mary. This victory by parliament is supposed to have checked the arbitrary exercise of power by the Crown, secured the rights of private property, limited taxation, and thereby created a favourable climate for investment. The Industrial Revolution was the inevitable result.

In the 18th century, Britain had a parliament controlled by large landowners, and it did pass many acts that provided for road improvements, the construction of canals, and the reorganization of agriculture. The new infrastructure probably boosted the economy.

Taxation, however, was high—not low—and the proceeds were used to fund the army and the Royal Navy, which secured Britain its colonial empire. The empire contributed to the Industrial Revolution, but not by strengthening the legal system as the enthusiasts for 1688 maintain. One reason was that Britain already had an effective legal system before 1688, and it underpinned the huge economic expansion that had taken place in the 16th and 17th centuries.

Some social scientists have argued that the cause of economic growth was the spread of a rationalistic culture that emphasized discipline and hard work. Max Weber linked this to Protestantism and the Reformation. Many English were Puritan Calvinists of the sort that Weber thought exemplified the Protestant Ethic, and the Scottish Presbyterian Church was even more avowedly Calvinist. However, English Puritanism was discredited in the Civil War as lower class radicals and democrats claimed divine inspiration for their demands. The upper classes shifted their religious stance toward Deism in the 18th century. This view imagines God as a retired engineer, who set the universe in motion according to Newton's laws and who has never subsequently intervened—either to cause miracles or to promote democratic doctrines.

The Scientific Revolution of the 17th century was, of course, a second source of Deism. Scientific discoveries did underpin some 18th-century technology, notably the steam engine, and may have promoted technological progress more generally by popularizing the scientific method. There was, indeed, much enthusiasm for science and technology among the upper classes. King George III received special tuition in science and had an impressive collection of apparatus for his laboratory exercises. Many of his subjects attended lectures and demonstrations put on in coffee houses. This activity may have made the Brits more sympathetic to technological progress.

It is not clear, however, if commitment to the scientific world view extended very far down the social scale. Belief in witchcraft, for instance, was widespread. In 1682, the brother of Lord Chief Justice North recalled that 'It is seldom that a poor old wretch is brought to trial' for witchcraft,

> but there is at the heels of her, a popular rage that does little less than demand her to be put to death; and if a judge...declare himself against the impious vulgar opinion, that the devil himself has power to torment and kill innocent children, or that he is pleased to divert himself with the good people's cheese, butter, pigs, and geese, and the like errors of the ignorant and foolish rabble

then the villagers 'cry this judge hath no religion, for he doth not believe [in] witches.' Enthusiasm for science may have been a film floating on a lake of superstition.

Triggering events

While the background factors sustained institutions, practices, and culture that supported technological innovation and business investment, they were not sufficient on their own to explain the Industrial Revolution. Other parts of the world were equally blessed, but they did not have industrial revolutions. Specific triggers were present in Britain that meant the Industrial Revolution happened there. We explore these in Chapters 2 and 3.

Chapter 2
The pre-Industrial Revolution, 1500–1700

Witney is a small market town 15 miles north-west of Oxford.
It is far from northern Britain where the Industrial Revolution
unfolded, but it nevertheless experienced many of the same
changes. Before looking at national and international patterns,
we will see what happened in Witney. It illustrates many themes
of both the pre-industrial and industrial revolutions.

A cloth industry grew up in Witney during the middle ages based
on Cotswold wool, water from the Windrush River for fulling
and dying, and good road connections to London via the New
Bridge and the Abingdon bridge built in the 15th century. By the
early 17th century, Witney was specializing in blankets, the
product for which it became famous. The market was international.
The highest quality blankets were exported to Spain and
Portugal. They were taken by wagon to London where they
were shipped overseas.

Poorer quality blankets went to North America. In the 18th
century, many were bought by the Hudson Bay Company and sent
to Canada where they were swapped for beaver pelts with the
native Indians. The Hudson Bay Company remained a major
purchaser of Witney blankets into the 19th century. Globalization
penetrated and transformed rural Oxfordshire (see Figure 3).

EARLY'S
ORIGINAL

WITNEY POINT
BLANKETS

MADE IN ENGLAND SINCE 1669
GUARANTEED ALL WOOL

3. Early's point blankets.

In the 18th century, the business was organized in the pre-industrial manner. There were sixty to eighty master weavers who owned, on average, three looms each. One they worked themselves, and the others were operated by other family members, apprentices, and journeymen hired for a wage. In 1712 the Witney Blanket Company was chartered. It operated as a traditional guild setting quality standards and regulating apprenticeships. All master weavers were required to be members. In 1721 a Hall was erected and served as the inspection point for blankets as well as for guild meetings. The master weavers subcontracted fulling and dying to other artisans and supplied women in outlying villages with raw wool which they carded and spun. Production fluctuated around 7,000 packs of wool per year.

During the Industrial Revolution, the technology changed and so did the organization of work. Around 1800, the spring loom was introduced. This loom with a flying shuttle could be operated by one man rather than two as was previously required. The spinning jenny was adapted to the coarse wool used for blankets, and the domestic spinners lost their jobs. On the organizational front, the number of master weavers dropped to less than a dozen. In 1838, the largest employer was John Early who employed seventy weavers and owned spinning and fulling machinery. The factory had arrived in Witney.

These changes did not benefit the workforce. Arthur Young, a renowned agricultural improver and commentator on all aspects of economic life, observed that mechanization meant that 'the masters and the fabric may flourish, but it cannot be contended that the labouring hands do the same.' The employment of weavers was cut in half. 'The effect of the introduction of machinery gave...the power of keeping down wages in such a manner as to deprive the poor of any share in, or at least leaving them a very small one in, that prosperity which has pervaded the kingdom.' Weavers earned nominally the same wage throughout the Industrial Revolution (11 shillings per week), but its purchasing power was much lower in 1830 than it had been in 1770 because consumer prices were 50 per cent higher. Much of the countryside was affected since factory spinning meant that the women were unemployed. William Cobbett wrote,

> A part, and perhaps a considerable part, of the decay and misery of this place [Whittington, Gloucestershire] is owing to the use of *machinery*...in the manufacture of blankets, of which fabric the town of Witney...was the centre, and from which town the wool used to be sent round to, and the yarn, or warp, come back from, all these Cotswold villages,...This work is all now gone, and so the women and girls are a 'surplus *popalashon, mon*'.

The decline in employment and real wages did mean that blankets could be profitably woven in Witney, and the industry remained the economic basis of the town for two more centuries. Technical progress continued. The first steam engine was erected for spinning in 1851, and steam power became general after the arrival of the railway in 1861. The power loom was applied to blanket making in 1858, a generation after its application to cotton. Investment in new technology was substantial after the Second World War, but it was not enough to sustain the industry. The successor to John Early's firm shut down, and the last blanket was woven in Witney in 2002. The 18th-century weavers' cottages and the blanket hall now comprise the Witney Conservation Area and are much sought after residences.

The rise of northern Europe

The growth of the Witney blanket industry in the 17th and 18th centuries is an example of a broader trend—the shift of manufacturing from the Mediterranean to north-western Europe. In 1500, at the end of the middle ages, Italy and Spain were the most urbanized countries and Europe's manufacturing power houses. The only comparably developed parts of north Europe were the Low Countries (modern day Belgium and the Netherlands).

Otherwise, the continent was largely rural and agricultural. These differences in economic structure are illustrated in Box 1, which divides the population into three sectors—urban, agricultural, and rural non-agricultural.

In 1500, the agricultural population made up three-quarters of the total in England and the large continental countries. (This is the same proportion that one observed in less developed countries like India and China early in the 20th century.) The percentage was lower in Italy, Spain, and the Low Countries. The latter had correspondingly larger urban populations, and that was important since most manufacturing took place in cities. The rural non-agricultural populations comprised a similar fraction of the population (14–19 per cent) in all of the European countries in 1500 and consisted of servants in country houses, priests, workers in transportation, and village craftsmen satisfying local needs.

Box 1 How did globalization transform pre-industrial Europe?

We can see how the economies of European countries were transformed between 1500 and 1750 by dividing people into three categories depending on where they lived and what they did. The categories are 'urban' (those living in settlements of more than 5,000 people), 'agricultural' (those living outside of urban settlements and farming the land), and 'rural, non-agriculture' (those living outside of urban settlements and doing jobs other than farming). Examples of the latter include the village clergy, monks, domestic servants, carters, miners, spinners, weavers, and other craftsmen. The table that follows shows these divisions for the principal European countries following modern boundaries. The percentages add up to 100 per cent for each country in each year. The countries that changed the most were the commercial powers of north-western Europe.

The Industrial Revolution

	1500			1750		
	Urban	Rural non-agriculture	Agriculture	Urban	Rural non-agriculture	Agriculture
Greatest transformation (%)						
England	7	18	74	23	32	45
Netherlands	30	14	56	36	22	42
Belgium	28	14	58	22	27	51
Slight evolution (%)						
Germany	8	18	73	9	27	64
France	9	18	73	13	26	61
Austria/Hungary	5	19	76	7	32	61
Poland	6	19	75	4	36	60
Little change (%)						
Italy	22	16	62	22	19	59
Spain	19	16	65	21	17	62

Source: Robert C. Allen, 'Economic Structure and Agricultural Productivity in Europe, 1300–1800', *European Review of Economic History*, 2000, Vol. 3, pp. 8–9.

By the eve of the Industrial Revolution, the centre of handicraft manufacturing in Europe had shifted to the North Sea. The English economy was the most transformed. The agricultural share of the population had dropped to 45 per cent, while the urban share jumped to 23 per cent, and the rural non-agricultural share leaped to 32 per cent—the highest percentage in Europe. Some of the growth in the urban share was due to an expansion in manufacturing (e.g. furniture making and book publishing in London; metal working in Birmingham; and so forth), but much of it was due to the growth of commerce and shipping. The growth of manufacturing was most apparent in the increase in the rural, non-agricultural share. In the 17th century, the wool and linen industries like many others expanded in the countryside. The Witney model was widespread: merchants signed up men and women to spin yarn, weave fabrics, and knit stockings in their homes. The merchant brought the raw material to the workers, collected the finished articles, and paid the spinners and weavers for their effort. These rural industries were geographically concentrated, and their products were sold across Europe and, indeed, around the world. England was a leader in this so-called 'proto-industrial' revolution.

The Dutch and the Belgians were not far behind. Indeed, the Dutch economy was the most modern, if not the most transformed, by the end of the 17th century. The Netherlands was the most urbanized and had the smallest share of its population in agriculture. The great question in early modern political economy was how to catch up with the Dutch. The British managed to do that with their Industrial Revolution.

The other countries in Europe were transformed to a much lesser degree. There was a small decline in the agricultural share of the workforce in the big continental countries and a corresponding increase in rural manufacturing, but the cities remained small. These were not the economic leaders.

The economies of Spain and Italy were the least transformed of all. The stasis is somewhat deceptive—the constancy in the Spanish urban share encompasses the huge growth of Madrid and the collapse of the old manufacturing cities. Nonetheless, Italy and Spain had slipped from first to last place in European economic performance.

Success in the global economy

Why were the economies of England and the Low Countries so radically transformed? The background factors highlighted in Chapter 1 made a contribution, but they were not sufficient. Indeed, many of these 'background factors' were arguably consequences of the expansion of north-western Europe, so causation is murky. The background factors, if they worked at all, did so by strengthening the responsiveness of the economy to incentives by either improving the 'climate of investment', the mobility of labour, or the attitudes of businessmen or by reducing the chance that progress would be swamped by demographic expansion. We can gain further insight into why the Industrial Revolution happened in Britain by analysing the evolution of the economic incentives themselves.

It was the evolution of the international economy and the imperial and military policies of the governments of Europe that created the peculiar incentives that triggered the Industrial Revolution. In the middle ages, pepper, cinnamon, nutmeg, and other spices were exported from India and South-East Asia to Europe via the Middle East. In the 15th century the invention of the square rigged ship allowed Europeans to sail around Africa to Asia. Vasco da Gama reached India in 1498, and his success led to the establishment of a Portuguese empire in Asia and Brazil. Success was short lived, however, for many of these Asian colonies were seized by the Dutch in the 16th century. Some years before Vasco da Gama's voyage, Christopher Columbus convinced King Ferdinand and Queen Isabella of Spain to fund his attempt to reach Asia by sailing west across the Atlantic, and he reached the Bahamas in 1492. The 'discovery' of America (the Grand Banks of Canada had been frequented by European fishermen for centuries) led to a scramble for colonies in which Spain looked the early winner, for the conquest of Mexico and Peru gave it vast quantities of silver. This treasure proved counterproductive for the economy, however, since it led to inflation that rendered Spanish agriculture and manufacturing uncompetitive. By the 17th century, England, France, and other powers were seizing colonies in the Caribbean, where fortunes were made in sugar plantations manned with African slaves. The English also established a string of colonies along the east coast of North America. (See Figure 4.)

Bengal was conquered by the English East Indies Company in 1757. The Dutch and the French also founded colonies in India, the Caribbean, and North America, but they were defeated by the English who took many of their colonies from them. The English and the French followed 'mercantilist' economic policies, and used tariffs and other trade restrictions to secure their colonial markets

4. A south-east view of the city of Boston, c.1730.

for themselves. As the English empire expanded, so did the market for English manufactured goods, and this led to the great expansion of rural manufacturing and urban employment shown in Box 1. Witney, as we saw, grew by exporting blankets to Canada.

Some knock-on effects

England's success in the global economy had important effects beyond the growth of cities and rural manufacturing. These include the agricultural revolution, the coal revolution, the high wage economy, and the expansion of literacy.

There was an agricultural revolution in England in the 17th and early 18th centuries—crucially before the Industrial Revolution: more bushels of grain were reaped per acre; cows gave more milk; and sheep, more wool and mutton. Output per worker also increased. This was the flip side of the declining share of the population in agriculture. In 1500 each person in agriculture supported him- or herself plus about one-third of a person off the farm. By 1750, one agricultural person supported him- or herself plus one and one-fifth in rural industry or the cities. The growth in agricultural labour productivity made it possible for the cities and rural industries to expand.

Causation ran the other way, however. It was long thought that the rise of capitalist agriculture led to an increase in production and a decline in farm employment that induced cities to grow by flooding them with cheap labour and food. In fact, causation began with the growth of Britain's empire and the mercantilist policies that excluded other countries from trading with its colonies and, instead, focused that trade onto Britain. The growth in trade led to the expansion of the urban and manufacturing economies. As London and the other cities grew, so did the demand for food and labour. Farmers responded by increasing production. As labour was sucked from the countryside, farm sizes were increased and land was converted to pasture, so agriculture could operate with fewer workers. Agriculture was revolutionized by the growth of empire.

The coal revolution was also a direct result of the growth of London. At the end of the middle ages, small amounts of coal were scratched from outcrops on all of the major British and European coal fields. Production did not increase, however, because wood remained relatively inexpensive. When London's population was only 50,000 in 1500, firewood and charcoal were secured close to the capital and transport costs were modest. As the city's population exploded in the next two centuries, the demand for fuel ballooned, and supplies travelled a much greater distance—and at much greater cost. The price of charcoal in London rose in the 16th century, pulling up the price of coal as well.

As wood became more expensive, consumers were tempted to use coal instead. Switching was not simple, however, because wood was the cleaner fuel. Coal contained sulphur, which had to be removed in many industrial processes. Sulphur also rendered coal unsatisfactory for residential heating and cooking, which were the major applications. The shift to coal required the invention of new technology to burn it. In the case of residential heating, an entirely new house had to be designed. The medieval house had a hearth in the centre of the main room where a fire was built. Smoke drifted up into the rafters and left the house through a vent in the roof. If coal were substituted for wood, the house would have filled with noxious fumes—if the fire burnt at all. In fact, it would have been difficult to burn coal in an open fire, for coal must be confined in a space with a strong draught to burn well.

The solution was the terraced house with back to back fireplaces venting up through a chimney built into the party wall. It took considerable experimentation in many new houses to work out the design and dimensions of these systems—how did you induce the smoke from the ground floor to rise through the chimney rather than exit through a first-floor fireplace? This experimentation was facilitated by the large-scale house construction in London, as it expanded in the 16th and 17th centuries.

When both fuels were sold in London in the 17th century, coal cost about half the price per unit of energy compared to firewood or charcoal. As London expanded in the 16th century, wood fuel prices rose. By the 1580s they reached a value that was high enough so that coal could be sold in London at a great enough price to cover the cost of mining it in Northumberland and shipping it to London. That is when the coal trade took off.

Once the coal industry was established, northern Britain had access to some of the cheapest energy in the world. In the early 18th century, coal sold in London at about 11 pence per million British thermal units (MBTUs), a unit of heat energy. The price of energy from peat was similar in Amsterdam, where British coal was also sold. Energy was much more expensive elsewhere. It cost 19 pence in Paris and 20 in Beijing. In Newcastle upon Tyne and other northern cities, on the other hand, energy only cost 1.5 pence per million MBTUs. The Industrial Revolution happened in those cities rather than in London. As it happens, the coal mines were also close to iron ore deposits, and that conjunction of resources led to the modern iron industry. The steam engine was developed to drain coal mines, and the first railed ways were constructed in collieries to bring out the coal. The early development of Britain's coal resources underpinned an essential trajectory of technological advance.

Wages and living standards

The growth of cities, manufacturing, and commerce also had a profound impact on the British labour market. Figure 5 charts the course of real wages and population in England from the middle ages through the 18th century.

The period divides neatly in two. In the first phase from 1300 to 1600 the economy was mainly agricultural. This period was

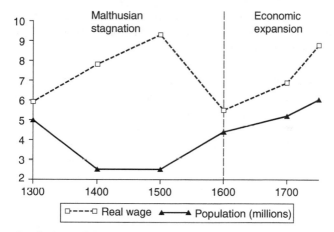

5. **Population and the real wage in England, 1300–1750.**

marked by Malthusian stagnation. When the population fell as it did in 1348/9 due to the Black Death, real wages increased in response to the scarcity of labour. When the population then rebounded as it did between 1500 and 1600, real wages dropped as labour was employed in lower and lower productivity tasks. There was no cumulative progress—only a cycle around bare subsistence. This pattern is typical of many pre-industrial economies.

After 1600, however, this pattern was broken—and that is the critical point. From 1600 to 1750, the British population grew steadily *and so did the real wage.* With the labour supply growing in these centuries, the wage could rise only if the demand for labour increased faster than the population. The demand for labour was growing due to the growth in cities and manufacturing, which, in turn, was due to Britain's growing commercial empire. Britain's pre-industrial economic growth led to rising real wages in Britain.

After 1600, British living standards began to pull ahead of those in the rest of the world. We can follow this development by comparing annual labour earnings to the cost of living, which is measured as the annual cost of a basket of consumer goods. Two examples are shown in Box 2.

In both baskets, the calorie consumption of the average person (averaging over men, women, and children) is set at 2,100 per day. The subsistence basket is typical of very poor people. Most expenditure is on the cheapest available grain—oatmeal in the British case—and it supplied most of the calories. The diet contains little meat and no alcohol. Non-food expenditures are low. Baskets like this using wheat flour or rice as the staple cost as much as the World Bank's famous $1-a-day poverty line.

The respectability basket, on the other hand, is what labourers in southern England aspired to. White bread replaced oatmeal, and there was meat and beer. The respectability basket cost at least twice as much as the subsistence basket.

Could a labourer buy enough of these baskets to support his family? We answer that question by dividing the earnings of a labourer, assumed to work full time, full year, by the annual cost of four baskets on the assumption that a family consisted of a father, mother, and two children. This 'subsistence ratio' is our measure of the real wage. A value of one indicates that a man earned just enough to keep his family at subsistence. Higher values indicate greater prosperity, while values less than one indicate crisis.

In 1770, a Witney weaver earned enough to buy almost three subsistence baskets, and, indeed, he earned enough to upgrade his standard of living to the respectability standard. If his wife spun part time, they made almost 50 per cent more than the cost of that basket. (By the 1820s this had all changed, for the wife had lost her spinning job, and the value of the man's earnings collapsed. They still had enough to buy the subsistence basket, but respectability was beyond their means.)

Box 2 How do we measure the standard of living?

We measure the standard of living as the annual income of a family divided by the cost of maintaining the family at a consumption level we set with a budget. Annual income either comes from a social table (see Boxes 5 and 6) or is estimated from a daily wage rate by assuming the person worked 250 days per year. Budgets defining the standard of living have been standardized. The 'respectability basket' and the 'bare bones subsistence basket' are shown here:

	Basket	
	Respectability: quantity per person per year	Bare bones subsistence: quantity per person per year
Oatmeal/grain		170 kg
Bread	182 kg	
Beans/peas	34 kg	20 kg
Meat	26 kg	5 kg
Butter/oil	5.2 kg	3 kg
Cheese	5.2 kg	
Eggs	5.2 kg	
Beer	182 litres	
Soap	2.6 kg	1.3 kg
Linen/cotton	5 metres	3 metres
Candles	2.6 kg	1.3 kg
Lamp oil	2.6 litres	1.3 lires
Fuel	5.0 MBTU	2.0 MBTU

(Cont.)

Box 2 Continued

The 'respectability basket' describes the consumption pattern of a respectable labourer in southern England in the 18th century. The 'bare bones subsistence basket' defines an austere standard of living that is the minimum needed for survival. The cheapest available grain is used in the calculation (for instance, oatmeal in Britain and maize in northern Italy), so bare bones subsistence baskets can be used to compare living standards around the globe. In both baskets the calorie level is set at 2,100 calories per day, and the quantity of grain is adjusted to ensure that outcome.

The table shows the yearly consumption of one person. Usually a family of four is assumed to have consumed four of these baskets, and the cost of those baskets is increased by 5 per cent to allow for rent when computing the family's annual cost of living. In this book when we refer to the cost of the basket, we mean the cost of the items in the table plus the rent allowance.

The ratio of the family's annual income to the cost of four baskets including the rent allowance is our measure of the standard of living. It indicates the number of baskets that the family can consume in a year. In practice, if they have a high income, they will upgrade their consumption pattern rather than spend all their money on the basic goods in the basket.

Figure 6 compares the real wages of labourers in leading European and Asian cities from the middle ages to the Industrial Revolution.

Real wages were similar across Europe after the Black Death, but then a great divergence emerged. Wages in London and Amsterdam remained high. Workers in those cities could buy several subsistence baskets for their families (although typically they upgraded their spending on food to include more meat, beer, etc.). In contrast real wages fell in Florence and Vienna.

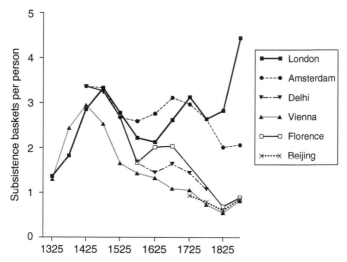

6. Wages relative to the cost of subsistence around the world.

By the 18th century labourers there could barely afford one subsistence basket. Workers in Beijing and Delhi received similarly miserable earnings. The difference between these cities was due to international trade. London and Amsterdam were booming ports and wages were very high. The population was growing rapidly as migrants were drawn in from the countryside. The demand for labour grew rapidly enough to sustain the high wage. In contrast, labour demand was static in most of continental Europe and Asia, so population growth drove wages down to subsistence. Britain's high wage economy had implications for many aspects of life during the early Industrial Revolution. One was consumption. Many fully employed British workers earned several times the subsistence level. They did not respond to this by buying several times the oatmeal shown in Box 2. Instead, they upgraded their consumption to the respectability basket. In addition, British workers purchased more manufactured goods—dishes, pictures, clothing, for instance. There was a consumer revolution in the 18th century, and British workers were in the thick of it.

Health and literacy

Well-being is based on more than just consumption. The United Nations Human Development Index combines income, health, and educational attainment to get a more balanced view. We can likewise broaden the comparisons for the pre-industrial period.

One of our best indicators for health is the height of adults. Since the 17th century, the average height of men has increased from perhaps 160 cm in many European countries to 180 cm in the USA and UK and 184 cm in the Netherlands. The increase in height is attributed to an improvement in the 'net nutritional status' of children, who do the growing. Net nutritional status equals the food intake of the child, which contributes to growth, less the nutrition that is needed for work, or to fight off and recover from illnesses. In the late 18th century, Britain was leading this upward advance.

According to military recruitment records, British men achieved an average height of 172 cm. In contrast, the average height of Italians dropped from 167 cm to 162 cm as their real incomes fell, and maize flour replaced wheat in their diets.

High wages also contributed to economic growth by increasing the skills and knowledge of the workforce. It is difficult to measure school attendance in the past consistently and comprehensively, but we make a stab at measuring literacy by studying the proportion of people who could sign their name to documents rather than simply make a mark. Box 3 summarizes the results of this indicator.

In 1500, literacy was low across Europe. Only in the cities could many people sign their name. By 1800 literacy had increased everywhere. The increases were greatest in north-western Europe. About two-thirds of the Dutch and half of the people in England

Box 3 How educated were Europeans?

There are no comprehensive statistics on schooling in pre-industrial Europe, but we can glean some information about educational attainment by counting how many people could sign their names to documents rather than make a mark. Many more people could sign in cities than in the countryside. Literacy was very low at the end of the middle ages and increased substantially by 1800. By the Industrial Revolution, it was common for boys to have a few years of education in a village school and then to learn a trade through an apprenticeship.

Many girls also received some schooling, but literacy was higher for men than for women. The averages that follow include both men and women:

Percentage of adult population that could sign its name

	1500	1800
England	6	53
Netherlands	10	68
Belgium	10	49
Germany	6	35
France	7	37
Austria/Hungary	6	21
Poland	6	21
Italy	9	22
Spain	9	20

Source: Robert C. Allen, *The British Industrial Revolution in Global Perspective*, 2009, p. 53.

and present day Belgium could sign their names. These regions were also leading in numeracy to judge by the precision with which people stated their ages. There are probably two reasons for this competence. First, England and the Low Countries were urbanized, commercial economies. It paid to be able to read and write in that environment (unlike on the farm), so there was a high demand for schooling in these countries. Second, schooling was not provided free by the state; it had to be acquired privately. Wages were high in north-western Europe, so parents had the financial means to educate their children.

Chapter 3

Why the Industrial Revolution was British

The Industrial Revolution was Britain's path breaking response to the challenges of the first globalization launched by the voyages of Vasco da Gama and Christopher Columbus.

There were several connections. First, the growth in world trade brought new products to Britain including Chinese porcelain and Indian cotton cloth. They were in high demand, and British firms sought to imitate them. Second, the growth in trade and empire opened new markets for British products, and the ensuing expansion of production and commerce generated unusually high wages and cheap energy. How to compete in that environment was the overriding engineering challenge that British industry so creatively met. Third, the commercial expansion and the rise in wages aided British industry in meeting the challenge of foreign competition by improving the health and strength of the workforce and by raising the returns to education and skill. The result was a rise in literacy, numeracy, and trade skills that underpinned the manufacturing sector.

The Industrial Revolution also drew strength from another source that had little to do with globalization—the Scientific Revolution of the 17th century. It contributed both new knowledge—in particular, the discovery of atmospheric pressure and the vacuum—and new attitudes and practices. People came to study the world, including technology, 'scientifically', and that approach brought rewards in the realm of invention. Breakthroughs were due to 'macro inventors', who thought outside of the box and created wholly novel technologies. The macro inventors were often leading scientists or were influenced and informed by them as students, associates, or friends. Many people were connected to the scientific vanguard through networks that diffused the knowledge and attitudes of the Enlightenment across a broad swath of British society, making it more technologically creative. The Royal Society, founded in 1660, was at the apex of this network, which also included provincial associations like Birmingham's Lunar Society as well as a myriad of coffee houses and similar venues where scientific demonstrations were performed. These communication channels, as well as the widely held belief that technology could be advanced by observation and reason, is referred to as the 'Industrial Enlightenment'. The formation of those networks and the adoption of those attitudes could, of course, have been responses to an increase in the profitability of invention, but proponents of the Industrial Enlightenment view of the Industrial Revolution see it as a cultural development whose origin lay in the Scientific Revolution and the broader Enlightenment rather than in economics.

Cotton

The cotton industry is a prime example of the transformative effect of Asian imports on the British economy. In the 17th century, the East India Company began shipping Indian calicos and muslins to England, and the fabrics were so popular that attempts were made to imitate them domestically. In the early 18th century, complicated and shifting import restrictions were introduced to protect the English woollen industry from Indian competition. These restrictions had the unintended consequence of creating a sheltered niche in which an English handicraft cotton industry could begin to operate. Its cloth was exported to Africa where it was bartered for slaves and competed against Indian calicos. English production remained small scale, however, until the production process was mechanized.

This got underway in the 1760s in spinning and printing but was not completed until the 1840s when the power loom drove the handloom out of business. By 1850, cotton employed one-sixth of the manufacturing workforce and accounted directly for 8 per cent of GDP. Eric Hobsbawm caught an important truth when he wrote 'whoever says industrial revolution says cotton'.

While the Industrial Enlightenment was present in the potteries and in the development of steam power, it was peripheral to the cotton industry, for the inventors in cotton were principally artisans without Enlightenment connections. Samuel Crompton (1753–1827), the inventor of mule spinning, was the son of a part-time farmer and weaver. While a youth, he was taught spinning and weaving. He attended school where he excelled in mathematics. This was typical of textile inventors and attests to the importance of widespread education. From the age of 16 he worked in secret for a decade to improve spinning machines. Apart from the textile trade, his activities were centred around the New Jerusalem Church, a Swedenborg congregation, rather than Enlightenment institutions.

Machinery was the secret of success in the cotton trade. It was developed in Britain in response to the country's high wages and gave Britain a competitive advantage for decades. The three main branches of the trade—spinning, weaving, and finishing—were all mechanized.

Once calico imports from India proved there was a market for cotton, hand spinning was begun. Merchants brought raw cotton to women who spun it on wheels in their cottages in return for wages (see Figure 7).

7. Irish cottage with handloom weaver and spinner.

The hours of labour to spin a pound (lb) of cotton increased with the fineness of the yarn. Wages were much higher in Britain than in India with the result that Britain could compete successfully with India only in the coarsest yarns, which required the least labour. To produce finer yarn, British firms needed to economize on labour, and that could only be done by inventing machines.

Many Britons responded to the chance to make a profit by trying to invent spinning machines. John Wyatt and Lewis Paul almost succeeded with roller spinning in the 1740s and 1750s, but their Birmingham mill ultimately went bust. James Hargreaves perfected his jenny in the mid-1760s, and it was the first successful machine. He was inspired by watching a spinning wheel rotate after it had fallen on its side. Afterwards, he contrived to run a row of vertical spindles off a common horizontal wheel using wooden clamps to pull the yarn in imitation of the spinner's fingers. In 1767, Richard Arkwright hired John Kay, a clockmaker, to make a machine using rollers, which took five years to perfect. Both Hargreaves and Arkwright also invented carding machines to prepare the cotton for spinning. Arkwright established a factory at Cromford to house his machines (see Figure 8).

He improved the layout when he built his second mill, and it became the prototype for cotton mills in Europe and the USA. A decade later, Crompton combined elements from Hargreaves' and Arkwright's designs to create the mule, which became the principal spinning machine in Britain in the 19th century. Once in operation, of course, the spinning machines were improved through 'learning by doing' as engineers observed their operation and perfected them. Hargreaves' and Arkwright's machinery made Britain the world's low cost producer of coarse yarn, and the mule made Britain the low cost producer of fine yarn as well.

A much debated question is why these inventions were made in England rather than in France or India. An economic explanation turns on wages and machinery prices. The first spinning machines

8. Factory spinning.

were an expensive way to save labour and not very good at it. In the late 18th century, spinners' wages were much lower relative to the price of equipment in both France and India than they were in Britain. The early spinning machines were profitable to use in Britain because the value of the labour they saved was high relative to the cost of the machine. They were not worth using on the continent or in India since the value of the labour they saved was very small relative to the cost of the equipment. Early spinning machines were profitable to use in Britain but not abroad, and that is why the Industrial Revolution was British.

History repeated itself in weaving. Hundreds of spinning mills were erected in the 1780s. The price of cotton yarn dropped sharply, and the weaving industry expanded to process all the yarn. Weaving, however, remained a cottage industry using traditional handlooms. Employment exploded, reaching a quarter million (10 per cent of the adult male workforce) in the early 19th century. As the labour market tightened, the wages of the weavers also leaped up, and the 1790s and first decades of the 19th century witnessed 'the golden age of the handloom weaver'. The Reverend Edmund Cartwright, the only cotton inventor with arguably Enlightenment connections—he came from a landed family, attended Magdalen College, Oxford, and was a member of the Society of Arts and the Board of Agriculture—thought it would be simple to design a weaving machine. He was inspired by automatons—the clockwork dolls that mimicked the movements of humans. If a mechanical woman could play a harpsichord, perhaps she could also weave calico? The task proved to be immensely complex. Cartwright wasted his family's fortune working on it for decades, and other inventors took up the challenge. It was not until the 1820s that the power loom was improved sufficiently to challenge the handloom weavers.

In both spinning and weaving, the cottage mode of production contained the seeds of its own destruction. When the cost and demand situation was favourable, the cottage mode responded with large increases in employment and output. As employment approached the limits of the available labour force, the earnings of people with the necessary skills rose, and those high wages became the target of inventors, for the high wages meant that even comparatively poorly designed machines could turn a profit.

Weaving was not the final stage in the manufacture of cloth. It had to be finished.

Much of the enthusiasm for Indian calicos in the 18th century stemmed from the brightly coloured designs that decorated the cloth. The English imitated the look with different methods. Indian cloth was usually hand painted, while the English used a more capital intensive approach. Initially patterns were printed from wood blocks with the result that 'the drawing of one clever designer could be reproduced by many less skilled workmen, whereas the Indian must both design and execute his own work'.

By the 1760s, copper plates had replaced the wooden blocks, but the latter were still general on the continent.

Numerous attempts were made to make the process continuous by printing from cylinders. Commercial success was achieved in 1783 with Thomas Bell's design.

The course of invention in all branches of the industry responded to the high wages earned by British workers in the 18th century. Wherever possible, the British opted for a more capital intensive method than the Indians employed. In Britain, the savings in labour costs outweighed the increase in capital costs since wages were high. That was not true in other countries with lower wages. As a result, machine technology cut production costs in Britain without conferring the same advantage on its competitors. The upshot was that by the 19th century, Britain had the most competitive cotton industry in the world.

Britain's share of world cotton textile production rose from a negligible fraction in 1750 to 30 per cent in 1880. Much of this expansion was at the expense of producers in Africa, the Middle East, and India.

The invention of the factory

Textile machinery was housed in mills, and cotton mills were the most common type of factory in Britain in the 1780s. Factories were hallmarks of the new age, for they implied many wage labourers working together on a single site rather than self-employed artisans toiling in their separate cottages. A centralized power source driving the machinery was one reason why production was concentrated, but it was not the only one. The division of labour, skill acquisition, supervision, and quality control were other considerations. The growth of the cotton industry gave a big boost to the factory, and the factory mode of production was adopted in many other industries as well, so it deserves a further look.

Making hats was an unglamorous industry that nonetheless achieved a high rate of productivity growth. This was achieved with the factory mode of production.

The Christy hat factory in Bermondsey in the early 1840s is a good illustration. The factory employed 1,500 people and was the largest hat factory in the world. This establishment 'well illustrates the economy of a large factory' in two respects. The first was effective organization—'the concentration of many departments within the walls of one establishment, the division of labour, the exercise of delegated authority by foremen to each department, and a general supervision of the whole by the proprietors'. The second source of high productivity was the use of machinery. The factory had a 10 horsepower (HP) steam engine that drove machines located around the site via a system of shafts and belts. Some tasks had been mechanized while others were done by hand and relied on the skill of the workers.

When wool entered the factory, it was washed—apparently by hand. Water was expelled, however, from the wool with a large screw press. The wool was dried and then it was carded with the kind of machine used in the textile industry. Likewise, furs were washed and their large hairs were removed. This was a hand operation.

> A number of women, seated on stools, are employed in pulling out the coarse outer hairs from the skins...Each woman lays a pelt on her lap, or on a low bench, and, by means of a knife acting against the thumb, tears out the larger hairs.

Next, the fur was removed from the pelts, again by women, but now operating power driven cutting machines that sliced off the hairs. The fine hair was separated from the coarse hair with a centrally powered blowing machine. A fan turned at 2,000 revolutions per minute, and the air blast carried the lighter fur further than the heavier fur, thus effecting the separation. The next step, in which wool and fur were turned into felt, depended on highly skilled labour rather than machinery. The materials were laid on the bench,

> and the bower, grasping the staff of the bow with his left hand, and plucking the cord with his right...causes the cord to vibrate rapidly against the wool and fur.... All the original clots or assemblages of filaments are perfectly opened and dilated, and the fibres, flying upwards when struck, are by the dexterity of the workman made to fall in nearly equable thickness on the bench, presenting a very light and soft layer of material

ready for felting. 'Simple as this operation appears to a stranger, years of practice are required for the attainment of proficiency in it.' The production process continued to alternate between highly skilled hand activities, less skilled activities, and machine processes until the hats were completed.

The Bermondsey factory illustrates the subdivision of production into a sequence of tasks requiring different degrees of skill, which were acquired through experience, and which were remunerated at different rates. Quality was checked by supervisors, and machinery was installed where a high capital labour ratio lowered costs. We know that the degree of mechanization was carefully thought out. In the 1830s, wages in the USA were already higher than in the UK, and American hat manufacturers had invented a more highly mechanized system than Christy's employed. Although Henry Christy was familiar with American technology from 1833 at the latest, his firm did not adopt the full-blown American system until the 1860s, in part, as he explained, because 'the rate of labour is much greater and the savings consequently greater' in the USA than in the UK.

Steam

Energy in the pre-industrial world came from the exertions of humans and animals, from burning organic fuels like firewood and charcoal, and from the power of wind and flowing water. Modern economic growth required more potent sources and the first to be harnessed was coal. Initially, it was burnt for heat in London in the late 16th century. In the 18th century, coal's thermal energy was converted to mechanical power through the steam engine. Pumping water out of mines was the first application. Engines were gradually improved in the next hundred years, but their economic impact was slight until the development of efficient, high pressure engines around the 1830s. These were applied widely to power industry and transportation. By the middle of the 19th century, the revolutionary potential of steam power was realized, and it made a significant contribution to economic growth.

The invention—and perfection—of the steam engine was closely connected to the Scientific Revolution, both in terms of the application of new knowledge and in terms of cultural and institutional connections to the scientific establishment. The wide availability of schools and technical training through apprenticeships were also important since the development of steam technology required many artisans and engineers from modest backgrounds.

The steam engine was an important application of knowledge discovered by 17th-century scientists. The science began with Galileo, who was the first to suspect that the atmosphere had weight. The idea occurred to him when he studied the problem of draining mines, and he noticed that suction pumps would not lift water more than about 30 feet. He got his secretary Evangelista Torricelli to work on this problem. Torricelli invented the mercury barometer and weighed the atmosphere. In 1672, von Guericke of Magdebourg weighed the atmosphere with a vertical cylinder containing a piston rising from the top of a cylinder. A rope was tied to the piston and looped over a pulley and held a platform on which van Guericke put weights. He found that by pumping the air out of the cylinder, the atmosphere pushed the piston down and raised the platform. He could offset that rise and weigh the atmosphere by putting weights on the platform. In 1675, Denis Papin eliminated the vacuum pump by filling the cylinder with steam and then condensing it. Papin had invented a proto-steam engine.

The von Guericke experiment was similar to the first successful steam engine invented by Thomas Newcomen in 1712 (see Figure 9).

Newcomen's engine also had a vertical cylinder and piston. Instead of the pulley, there was a balance beam, and the weights were replaced with a pump to drain water from a mine. By filling the cylinder with steam and then condensing it with a squirt of cold water—Newcomen's famous 'cold water injection'—the atmosphere pushed the piston down and raised the pump. Newcomen had found a way to raise water—and make money—from the weight of the atmosphere.

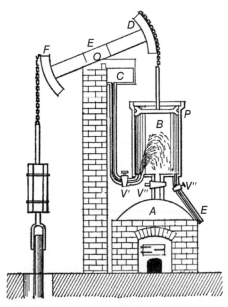

9. Diagram of Newcomen steam engine.

At one time, historians of the steam engine thought that Newcomen was wholly innocent of the science of the atmosphere, but in recent years that view has shifted, and it is now recognized that Newcomen probably did know what natural philosophers had discovered. The conduit was Thomas Savery, Fellow of the Royal Society, who knew the science. Savery invented a steam pump and visited Dartmouth to promote it. He probably met Newcomen there. They certainly had at least one friend in common. So it is likely that one of the greatest inventions of the Industrial Revolution really was science in action.

The science underlying the steam engine was pan-European (the leading scientists were Italians, Germans, and French), but the research and development (R&D) was carried out in Britain by an Englishman. The reason is that Britain was the only place where it was profitable to use the engine on a large scale, for two reasons. First, the main use of the engine was to drain mines, and Britain had the largest mining industry in Europe thanks to coal. Second, the engine used prodigious amounts of fuel, and coal mines offered cheap fuel. John Theophilus Desaguliers, a leading engineer in the early 18th century, observed:

> where there is no water [for power] to be had, and coals are cheap, the Engine now call'd the Fire Engine, or the Engine to raise the Water by Fire, is the best and most effectual. But it is especially of immense service (so as to be now of general use) in the Coal-Works, where the Power of the Fire is made from the Refuse of the Coals, which would not otherwise be sold.

The reason it was profitable to develop the Newcomen engine in Britain was because there were coal mines to be drained.

Newcomen's engine was the macro invention that began a technological trajectory.

In the next century and a half, the engine was perfected by many of the most famous engineers of the Industrial Revolution.

Consumption of all inputs was reduced including coal, which was cheap in Britain. Fuel consumption dropped from 44 lbs of coal per HP-hour in 1727 to 3 lbs in 1847. This improvement was a triumph for British engineering, although it undermined the country's competitive advantage by turning the steam engine, which had mainly benefited Britain in the 18th century, into a technology that could be used anywhere in the world. Once the coal consumption was reduced to 3 lbs per HP-hour, the price of coal was of little importance to the commercial application of the engine. British engineers had invented the 'appropriate technology' for everyone else.

An intellectual result of the Industrial Revolution was the image of the inventor as an Inspired Genius. This was no accident: middle-class propagandists promoted James Watt as a genius of invention—and, thus, a guarantor of the nation's prosperity—as a counter to the military genius of the Duke of Wellington, who not only defeated Napoleon but then became the political leader of the landed classes. In fact, invention occurred in many ways besides a genius having a brilliant idea. Much of invention consisted of painstaking engineering that turned often banal ideas into products or processes that worked reliably and cheaply. This was certainly the case in textiles. Thomas Edison's quip that 'invention was 1% inspiration and 99% perspiration' contained an essential truth. 'Learning by doing' was also important as engineers and managers observed how machines and production processes worked in practice and found ways to improve them. Sometimes businesses exchanged information (intentionally or otherwise) so that the advances made by one firm could be carried forward by another. The result was collective invention.

The history of the steam engine illustrates the different ways in which invention can be organized, and the importance of both the elite inventors of the Enlightenment and artisan inventors without connections to high level science. The steam engine was invented by Newcomen, a Dartmouth ironmonger, who did secure a patent in conjunction with Thomas Savery, FRS (Fellow of the Royal Society), to realize some gain. Fuel consumption fell from 44 lbs per HP-hour in 1727 to 30 lbs per HP-hour in 1769, probably because of collective invention as operators shared their results and built on each other's experience.

Consumption dropped again from 30 lbs to 17 lbs. This was the result of research by John Smeaton, FRS. Smeaton collected the records of fifteen engines—their owners did not keep them secret—and analysed them to determine the most efficient design. Smeaton did not patent his findings. He profited from his research through consulting contracts. Smeaton was a leading light in the Industrial Enlightenment.

The next advance was due to James Watt, FRS, whose famous separate condenser cut fuel consumption from 17 to 9 lbs. The first engine with a separate condenser went into service in 1776. Watt was certainly motivated by personal gain and obtained a patent on his condenser in 1769. Watt's career illustrates the two-fold nature of patents: it provided him with a reward for invention, but it also stifled later progress since he used his patent to prevent other inventors from experimenting with compounding cylinders. Engineering progress was retarded until Watt's patent expired in 1800.

Watt is also an example of the importance of social connections linking scientists and practical engineers. Watt was born in Greenock and was sent to Glasgow at the age of 18 to learn the trade of mathematical instrument maker. He stayed initially with his mother's family, and it was through her relative George Muirhead that Watt was introduced to members of Glasgow's scientific and cultural elite. He became a close friend of Robert Dick, future Professor of Natural Philosophy, and Dr Joseph Black, Professor of Medicine.

After a year's training as an instrument maker in London, Watt returned to Glasgow in 1757 and was allowed to open a workshop at the university where he made instruments for Joseph Black. Black's scientific research concerned heat, and he conceived the concept of 'latent heat', which he offered to Watt as an explanation for the success of his separate condenser.

Later Black took a chair at Edinburgh and set himself the task of developing the Scottish economy by applying scientific knowledge. He worked with industrial entrepreneurs. Black became a lifelong friend of Watt. Watt raised capital for his business ventures by forming partnerships with Black and other members of Black's circle like John Roebuck, who also hired him to erect one of his first steam engines at a coal mine in Kinneil. The Scottish scientific-industrial complex is the premier example of the Industrial Enlightenment, and Watt took advantage of its connections to deepen his ideas and further his inventions.

The next advance in steam power was effected by Cornish engineers who designed the famous Cornish pumping engines to drain copper and tin mines. Their goal was to save fuel, which was very expensive since coal was brought from South Wales. The problem was heightened by the expiry of Watt's patent in 1800, for Watt then withdrew his engineers from Cornwall, and engine efficiency dropped sharply. The mine owners did not want to pay Watt for advice, so they banded together to solve their problems themselves. Details of design and fuel consumption for all engines were ascertained monthly and published in *Lean's Engine Reporter*. In that way, engineers could learn from each other's experience, and Cornish engines were perfected over the next decades. This was collective invention on a grand scale, and it created the most efficient pumping technology ever seen. Patents were not necessary for progress. The engineers who accomplished these improvements did it without Enlightenment connections.

Ceramics

Porcelain is a prime example of the way in which Asian imports stimulated the Industrial Revolution. In the medieval and early modern eras, China had a large porcelain industry that exported exquisite vases, platters, and other goods around the world. Many of these were decorated with blue patterns on a white background, although other colours were also used. Porcelain production was initiated in England in the mid-18th century.

Starting a ceramics industry in a new country at that time was technically difficult since chemistry was in its infancy, which meant that the properties of the local raw materials could not easily be determined nor could the production methods be adapted through routine scientific methods. Knowledge of these matters was tacit and embodied in the artisans in the industry. These challenges were met through a stream of improvements starting in the mid-17th century. After foreign products were successfully imitated, progress was pushed forward by both famous and less well known potters.

The history of ceramics also lends support to the Industrial Enlightenment view that the advance of science gave impetus to technical progress through contacts with leading scientists and (more importantly) through the application of the scientific method to the perfection of manufacturing methods. Indeed, ceramics was one of the first industries in which modern, scientific knowledge replaced the artisan's tacit understanding.

In the mid-17th century, English ceramic production was in a primitive state. Most domestic production was cheap, locally produced earthenware. High end demand was met with imports of Chinese porcelain, and substantial quantities of salt glazed stoneware were imported from the Rhineland and sold to middle and lower class households.

The first steps towards establishing a British industry were taken by John Dwight (1633–1703), who is an excellent example of the Industrial Enlightenment pushing technology forward. Dwight was the son of a yeoman but had such academic promise that he was admitted to Oxford University where he studied law and chemistry, and worked in Robert Boyle's laboratory. He took his degree in law, however, and worked as an ecclesiastical official until 1669 when 'having tryed many experiments he concluded he had the secret of making China Ware. Thereupon he sold his [clerical] Office, came to London, was encouraged therein by Mr Boyl and Dr Hook.' He tried to manufacture all types of pottery imported into Britain. While he was unsuccessful in producing porcelain, his experiments unlocked the secret of manufacturing salt glazed stoneware. This was no mean achievement since it required the identification of suitable raw materials, the invention of a high temperature furnace, and discovery of the correct method of applying the salt glaze. Dwight patented his process and tried to keep it secret but was unsuccessful as his employees quit and founded competing firms. Dwight was responsible for the establishment of the salt glazed stoneware industry in England.

China exported porcelain across Eurasia, and people in many countries tried to produce it locally. The Ottoman Turks, for instance, made a fritware imitation. In the 15th century, potters in Iznik created a novel process using local materials that featured doubly fired cobalt blue patterns on a white underglaze. In the next two centuries, they expanded the colour range and exported large quantities to the Middle East and Europe. In the 18th century, however, the industry slid into decline without sparking an industrial revolution. In Europe, August the Strong, Elector of Saxony, was an avid porcelain collector and promoted research by Ehrenfried Walther von Tschirnhaus (another example of the Industrial Enlightenment, although a German) and the imprisoned alchemist Johann Friedrich Böttger. In 1708, they succeeded in making true porcelain, Saxon sources of

China stone and China clay were discovered, and the Meissen industry was born.

In England, it was another exemplar of the scientific culture, William Cookworthy (1705–80), who finally succeeded in producing hard paste porcelain. He was a successful apothecary. In the 1740s, he discovered deposits of China stone and China clay in Cornwall on land owned by Thomas Pitt, nephew of William Pitt the Elder and later First Baron Camelford. Pitt was not notable for his scientific interests, but he did finance Cookworthy's patent application and the experimental work to perfect the manufacturing process—presumably to raise the value of the minerals on his estate. Cookworthy had numerous scientific acquaintances including John Smeaton, who lodged in his house while building the Eddystone lighthouse (1756–9) and Captain James Cook and Joseph Banks, who dined with him in 1768.

Josiah Wedgwood (1730–95) was another paradigm of the Industrial Enlightenment, and he took English manufacturing to even higher levels of sophistication. His family were potters, and he was apprenticed to the trade. Nonetheless, he picked up the scientific idea that knowledge was gained though experiments, and he conducted 5,000 to find better materials and processes. He invented a pyrometer to measure temperatures more accurately, which led to his election to the Royal Society. He established a successful manufacturing business and led the industry in introducing new products like Queen's ware (an improved creamware), basalt ware, and jasper ware. As well as tableware, he produced medallions, ornaments, and vases. He was a great marketeer.

Dwight, Cookworthy, Wedgwood...This looks like the Industrial Enlightenment in action. However, while these luminaries made decisive contributions to the development of English pottery, they were not alone. The set of inventors was broader in two respects.

First, many inventions were made by people with only trades backgrounds and without Enlightenment connections. Wedgwood made his early money selling creamware, which became a staple of the English potteries for a century. Creamware was invented by Enoch Booth in the 1740s. Booth was the son of a butcher and apprenticed to a potter. Booth also invented the double firing process around 1750. He was the first to glaze a pot, fire it, paint a picture on the surface, and then fire the pot again with a clear glaze on the exterior to protect the image. Another inventor from a humble background was Josiah Spode I (his grandfather was a 'coal getter') who apprenticed with Thomas Whieldon. Spode perfected under glaze transfer printing in 1784 and developed bone china, a project that was finished by his son Josiah II. The famous inventors like Dwight and Wedgwood worked in an industry made up of independent artisan producers many of whom were making equally valuable contributions to technical progress. Indeed, one might try to subvert the Industrial Enlightenment by reclaiming Wedgwood for the artisans. He was, after all, engaged in his experiments on ceramics when he was only 24 years old and working with Thomas Whieldon. Wedgwood did not read his first paper to the Royal Society until he was 52. From the point of view of the artisans, the Royal Society showed good taste in celebrating one of their leading lights, but the impetus for his discoveries and achievements came from below, not from above.

Second, pottery technology developed through collective learning as well as through the efforts of inspired geniuses and R&D entrepreneurs. While artisans often tried to keep their improvements secret, this proved difficult since employees took the knowledge with them when they left the firm. The result was collective invention despite the efforts to suppress it. Technological progress in ceramics did not depend exclusively on the deeds of leading figures. The pervasiveness of collective invention is a second qualification that must be made to the inspired genius model as applied to the potteries.

It was one thing to design pretty pots, but it was another to make them cheaply.

Innovation in pottery was directed as much towards the latter as the former. England developed methods that differed fundamentally from those used in China. In both countries, technology evolved in the direction of reducing the use of expensive inputs while increasing the use of cheap ones. First, English manufacturers reduced the employment of skilled labour by adapting machinery developed for other industries. Wedgwood, for instance, installed lathes to turn the cylindrical parts of vases. Second, transfer printing was invented. In China artists painted the design on each piece. This was the first system used in England. It was very expensive. Transfer printing cut costs in England by substituting capital for labour. In transfer printing the design was engraved on a copper plate, which was then used to print the pattern on tissue sheets. While the ink was still wet, a sheet was laid on a previously glazed pot to which the ink then adhered, transferring the design to the pot. John Sadler, an English printer, and John Brooks, an Irish engraver, independently invented the process in the 1740s. The ink, however, wore off. The solution was to apply a second layer of glaze over the ink image and fire the pot again. John Wall, a physician and founder of the Worcester Porcelain Company, developed transfer printing with blue ink under glaze in 1757, and John Spode refined the technique, as noted, in 1784. The famous blue-on-white willow pattern, first engraved by Thomas Minton in 1780, was a transfer print (see Figure 10).

Third, although capital was substituted for expensive labour in the English potteries, it was not used indiscriminately, as a comparison of English and Chinese kilns shows.

English kilns were built to economize on capital and were profligate in their use of energy. English-style kilns had a coal fire in the bottom. The heat rose, enveloped the pots, and then vented out of the furnace through a hole in the top. Much of the energy

10. Plate decorated in willow pattern.

was wasted. The English kiln was cheap to build but not thermally efficient. In contrast, the Chinese kilns used lots of capital to preserve energy. They consisted of a series of chambers rising up a hillside. A fire burned at the entrance to the lower chamber where the heat was drawn in to bake the pots. The heat was not vented out of a hole in the top in the English manner. Instead, it was forced down through a hole at floor level and entered the next chamber up the hill. The heat was reused in chamber after chamber, so it was not wasted. This design, of course, equated to more capital. Pottery kilns, therefore, are another example of the way in which technology was designed in response to the cost of capital, fuel, and labour. In this case, expensive fuel in China led to the substitution of capital for energy, in contrast to English practice.

The final avenue by which the English cut costs was in the growth of factory production in the potteries. Wedgwood's Etruria mill was a leader. It was based on the division of labour, but, unlike cotton weaving mills, the aim was less to substitute unskilled women and children for male artisans, and more to upgrade skills by training people for artistic jobs. In addition, machinery was used, as noted, to raise labour productivity in tasks that could be done by lathes, for instance. Finally, inspection and quality control were obsessions.

The end of the Industrial Revolution

In some accounts, the Industrial Revolution ended around 1830, but in our view it had another generation to run. The progress achieved by 1830 was far from balanced. The cotton industry was very large; spinning was wholly mechanized; and the power loom was forcing the handloom onto the scrap heap of history. The technology of iron production had also been revolutionized, and an engineering industry had developed that supplied machinery mainly to the textile industry. There was some progress outside of these sectors—machinery was used in the production of candles and hats, as we have seen—but much of the economy was as yet untouched.

This situation changed between 1830 and 1870 as modern technology spread across the economy. An important indicator was the growing use of steam. At the beginning of the 19th century, most steam engines were installed in mines for draining. Industry was powered by water. In 1830, steam and water were equally important sources of power with 165,000 HP of each. By 1870, water power had increased to 230,000 HP while steam leaped to 2,060,000 HP. The increased use of steam was due to better fuel efficiency and the development of high pressure engines which were lighter and cheaper than the low pressure engines of Newcomen and Watt.

One advantage of a steam engine was that it was potentially mobile, unlike a water wheel. All early experimenters with high pressure steam tried to power a vehicle, but the results were unsatisfactory due to the poor condition of the roads. One solution was to put the engine on the rails commonly used to bring coal and ore out of mines. Richard Trevithick built the first steam locomotive that hauled minerals on the tramway of the Penydarren Ironworks in Wales in 1804. There was a market for locomotives in colleries, and their designs were gradually improved as engineers tried out alternative configurations and learned from experience. The great turning point was George and Robert Stephenson's *Rocket*, which won the Rainhill trials in 1829. They were awarded the locomotive contract for the Liverpool and Manchester Railway, which was the first general purpose railway and inaugurated a frenzy of construction. By 1867, 12,000 miles of track were in operation.

Railways were laid around the world and contributed to the integration of world markets.

Another solution to the problem of bad roads was to put the engine on a boat. Robert Fulton built the first commercially successful steam ship, the *Clermont*, which sailed the Hudson River in 1807. Crossing oceans was a bigger challenge. An issue was, again, the thermal efficiency of the engines, for a ship had to carry the coal it needed for its voyage, so the less efficient the engine, the more carrying capacity had to be devoted to coal rather than freight, which would bring in revenue. Isambard Kingdom Brunel's *Great Western* established that a ship could cross the Atlantic in 1838 and his *Great Britain* was the first iron ship driven by a screw propeller. The transition from sail to steam was gradual and depended on improvements in engine efficiency.

By the end of the 19th century, steam finally replaced sail on the longest route from Britain to China. As steam use increased, so did the integration of the world economy.

Between 1830 and 1870, steam driven machinery displaced human and animal labour in activities across the economy. Portable steam engines drawn by horses provided power on farms in the 1850s and were superseded by the traction engine (1859). In 1865 it was equipped with a roller and was used for road surfacing. Steam powered sawmills were replacing two men and a saw from the 1820s onwards. The pug mill replaced heavy manual labour in the mixing of clay for brick making and pottery. Bricks were formed with mechanical extruders rather than by hand. And so forth in industry after industry.

Steam power contributed very little to the growth in aggregate labour productivity before 1840. The greatest contribution came between 1850 and 1870, and coincided with the construction of railways and the spread of factories and machines across the range of British industries. Hand work disappeared and was replaced by higher productivity, higher paid factory work in the middle years of the 19th century.

Chapter 4
The condition of England

The last chapter was about the benevolent face of the Industrial Revolution. Now we turn our gaze to its dark side and consider why this upswing in technological progress caused such widespread suffering for so many people for so long. We begin with a broad question: how did the technological revolution change the structure of society?

Class structure

We can answer the question with social tables. A social table divides society into status or occupational groups, and the number of households in each group and their average incomes are specified. Gregory King prepared the first table for England in 1688. It was well-known and defined the genre. Massie updated King's table in 1759, Colquhoun revised it extensively to describe England as revealed by the first census in 1801 (although I date his table to 1798), and Smee and Baxter made further revisions using the occupational data in the censuses of 1841 and 1861, as well as information from income tax returns. Since investigators relied on varying sources of information and employed different occupational breakdowns, comparison across tables is not simple. Historians have addressed this problem by amending the tables with recently compiled information on the occupational distributions and the incomes, etc. Exact comparability is unlikely, but social tables do reveal major trends in the evolution of society.

Box 4 summarizes the major social tables by reducing the various occupations and statuses to six groups that can be traced across the Industrial Revolution.

The 18th-century tables did not include Scotland, and this specification has been continued throughout to ensure consistency. This is unfortunate; however, calculations with 19th-century data show that the ratios for Great Britain differ very little from those for England and Wales shown here.

The 'landed classes' formed the top group, owning most of the land in England, and agricultural rent formed the bulk of their income. Like all of the groups, this one was diverse. It included the king or queen, the peers of the realm, the gentry, and also the parish clergy of the Church of England, who were supported by glebe estates. The landowners also included the small number of university fellows who were supported by college properties. The landed classes were never more than 2 per cent of the population, and the proportion stayed roughly constant over time. The increase from 30,000 to 50,000 shown in Box 4 probably reflects the inclusion of female property owners in 1846 and 1867 who had been left out of the earlier counts. The landed classes were the wealthiest group in the country.

Box 4 How did England's social structure change over the Industrial Revolution?

In the table that follows, the English population is divided into six classes that can be followed from Gregory King's social table for 1688 to Dudley Baxter's table for 1867. The table shows the number of households (called 'families' in the early social tables) in each category in each year. Households included servants as well as related individuals. The landed class, that owned most of the real

(Cont.)

Box 4 Continued

estate in the country, was always small. The working classes were always the largest, and grew immensely during the Industrial Revolution. The middle classes, however, grew even faster. The number of farmers declined relative to the other groups as industry expanded. Paupers increased in number during the 18th century, and then declined slightly as industry grew, and the Poor Law was made more stringent.

	1688	1759	1798	1846	1867
A. Number of families or households					
Landed	31,626	29,070	38,704	52,986	50,695
Bourgeoisie	60,128	84,000	95,879	363,932	436,493
Lower middle	114,602	188,000	252,640	649,396	884,450
Farmers	402,440	379,008	320,000	243,130	223,271
Workers	980,863	1,128,247	1,804,567	2,598,299	3,668,936
Cottagers & paupers	161,672	192,310	439,897	320,648	317,726
Total	1,751,331	2,000,635	2,951,687	4,228,393	5,581,571
B. Distribution of families or households (%)					
Landed	1.8	1.5	1.3	1.3	0.9
Bourgeoisie	3.4	4.2	3.2	8.6	7.8
Lower middle	6.5	9.4	8.6	15.4	15.8
Farmers	23.0	18.9	10.8	5.7	4.0
Workers	56.0	56.4	61.1	61.4	65.7
Cottagers & paupers	9.2	9.6	14.9	7.6	5.7

Source: Robert C. Allen, 'Revising England's Social Tables Once Again', *Oxford University, Working Papers in Economic and Social History*, Number 146, 2016.

The next richest group was the 'bourgeoisie', which included the large-scale capitalists, bankers, merchants, lawyers, high officials, and investors. They already outnumbered the landed classes in 1688, and their number grew seven-fold during the Industrial Revolution. Their share of the population increased from 3 per cent to about 8–9 per cent over the period.

The third group was the lower middle class. In the 18th century, they were overwhelmingly shopkeepers and tradesmen. Typically, their businesses involved manufacturing as well as selling. They were 'the butcher, the baker, the candle-stick maker'. The lower middle class also included teachers, and in 1800 Colquhoun recognized another occupation—clerks. As the Industrial Revolution unfolded, more and more professional, educational, supervisory, and other salaried 'white collar' jobs were created. This category increased almost eight-fold from 1688 to 1867.

The fourth group, farmers, formed a declining share of the population. In 1688 there were close to 200,000 smallholdings held by husbandmen and yeoman, and cultivated by them and their families. The other 200,000 were larger farms mainly leased from great estates and cultivated by hired labour. The number of farms declined in the 18th and early 19th centuries as yeoman holdings were amalgamated into large farms. Agriculture was a declining sector during the Industrial Revolution.

The fifth group was the largest—workers. In the 18th century, they included servants, who were hired by the year and lived with their employers, labourers hired by the day, and many craft workers, who were usually paid by the piece or the job, and merged into independent contractors. Many of the artisans worked in their cottages. The Witney weavers are an example. Building workers, miners, and sailors, of course, worked on sites away from home. There were as many jobs in agriculture as in the rest of the economy.

This 'manual working class' was the largest group in the English economy. It grew by a factor of almost four during the Industrial Revolution. Most of the new jobs were non-agricultural. The character of work changed significantly as the independent craftsman working with hand equipment in his or her cottage gave way to machine operators employed in the new factories.

The poorest group were only partially employed, if they worked at all. In 1688 this group comprised almost one-tenth of the families. King referred to them as 'cottagers and paupers'. King put their incomes at subsistence, which means they were probably not working full time. In the 19th century, the poor were those who received poor relief. The share of the population who were paupers was constant to 1759 and then increased as the population expanded, the employment opportunities for women as spinners declined, and food prices rose as agricultural output lagged behind population. The decline in the number of poor shown in the table between 1798 and 1846 is the consequence of reforms to the Poor Law, which made it harder to get relief. The decline was thus spurious. However, the further decline to 1867 in the fraction who were poor probably reflected a rising demand for labour.

We can also use the social tables to track the incomes of these groups. This can be done either in terms of earnings or purchasing power. Box 5 shows the average income of an *earner* in each group.

Households could, and did, have multiple earners, for instance, when the husband wove, his wife spun, and their son toiled in a mill. The standard of living implied by these earnings depended on the prices of the goods that people consumed. There are many ways to measure those prices, and here we measure them as the cost of a basket of subsistence goods defined earlier. Dividing earnings per *person* in the household by the cost of the basket adjusts earnings for price changes and shows how many baskets each person could consume in a year (Box 6).

Box 5 How much did people earn?

There was at least one person in each household who brought in some money, and often there was more than one. 'Earners' in this sense were people who worked for wages or salaries, ran businesses, received dividends, interest on investments, rents from lands that they leased out, or poor relief. The incomes in the table that follows equal the total income earned by the class divided by the total number of earners in the class.

Average annual income per earner in £s

	1688	1759	1798	1846	1867
Landed	271.49	452.78	756.49	603.93	678.57
Bourgeoisie	175.38	145.37	525.45	441.23	466.29
Lower middle	24.47	27.17	64.79	111.64	75.00
Farmers	15.89	21.57	48.75	121.39	159.22
Workers	12.59	13.58	22.68	26.31	31.83
Cottagers & paupers	3.15	3.62	3.67	5.31	7.20
Average	19.91	23.14	40.29	57.30	65.66

Source: Robert C. Allen, 'Revising England's Social Tables Once Again', *Oxford University, Working Papers in Economic and Social History*, Number 146, 2016.

The condition of England

Throughout the period, the highest earning group were the landed classes. This privileged circle spanned the range from Jane Austen's Mr Darcy, with an income of £10,000 per year, which would have been near the apex of English society, to Mr Collins, the distasteful vicar, who took in perhaps £120. By the 1860s, Box 5 probably understates the income of this group since it assumes they were only receiving agricultural rent, and thus it

Box 6 How high was the standard of living and did it rise?

The standard of living is measured by 'real income'. First, income per person is calculated by dividing the total income of each class in each year by the total number of people in the class, including men, women, and children. The result is called 'nominal income per person'. 'Nominal income' is converted to 'real income' by dividing it by the cost of the subsistence basket defined in Box 2. The result is the number of subsistence baskets that each person in each class could buy in each year. In 1688, that ranged from just over one for cottagers and paupers up to almost thirty-one for the average member of the landed classes. The latter did not consume thirty-one times the amount of oatmeal porridge in the subsistence basket. Some of those baskets were used to hire servants, builders, and craftsmen. Others were traded up for better quality food and fine clothing. Over the Industrial Revolution, the average person's consumption more than doubled. All of the social classes gained, although by different amounts. Workers did not gain, on average, during the first half of the 19th century, but their real incomes jumped up after 1846.

Average real annual income per person (multiples of subsistence income)

	1688	1759	1798	1846	1867
Landed	30.92	45.42	53.57	49.97	50.98
Bourgeoisie	20.58	14.74	37.16	32.43	51.39
Lower middle	5.26	5.19	8.40	12.74	7.25
Farmers	3.80	4.50	6.89	10.91	11.96
Workers	3.27	3.27	4.39	4.37	6.21
Cottagers & paupers	1.02	1.02	1.17	1.98	2.43
Average	4.90	5.16	7.77	9.43	11.07

Source: Robert C. Allen, 'Revising England's Social Tables Once Again', *Oxford University, Working Papers in Economic and Social History*, Number 146, 2016.

excludes their earnings on urban property and non-agricultural investments, which were becoming important.

Box 6 shows how real incomes changed over the Industrial Revolution. The landed classes were always well off. They could consume thirty baskets each in 1688, and their consumption possibilities increased to fifty in 1800 after which they remained stable. In reality, no one consumed fifty times the quantity of oatmeal shown in Box 6. They upgraded their food consumption to more expensive sources of calories like quail and port, and hired builders, servants, and jewellery makers, who effectively ate their baskets (or upgraded versions) for them.

The landed classes consumed at a high level across the Industrial Revolution, but their relative position slowly eroded as agriculture declined vis-à-vis industry. In 1688 the agricultural rent received by the landed classes amounted to 16 per cent of the national income. By 1867, their rental income had dropped to 5 per cent.

The bourgeoisie were the second richest group. They were not far behind the landed classes. Their highest nominal incomes were, like those of the landed classes, realized in 1798, but they did not suffer in later years since the decline in monetary incomes was generally offset by lower prices. Sir Richard Arkwright, the entrepreneur and inventor of the water frame, earned about £20,000 per year (judging by his wealth at death) and his son raised that income to perhaps £40,000 (see Figure 11). He was reputed to be the richest commoner in the kingdom. In terms of consumption possibilities, the bourgeoisie had only twenty baskets per person in 1688 but did even better than the landed classes, slightly surpassing them (51.39 baskets versus 50.98) in 1867.

The incomes of the lower middle class and the farmers lay between those of the upper classes and the workers. In the 18th century, the average member of the lower middle class earned at least twice as

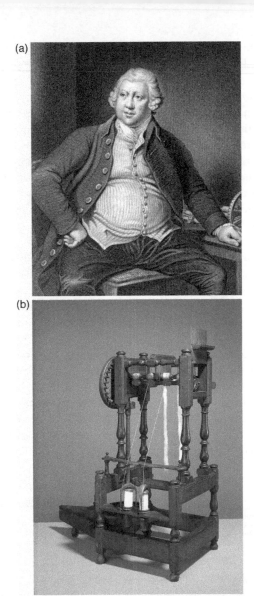

11. Richard Arkwright and his water frame.

much as the average worker. In 1688, the category of farmers earned only a quarter more than the workers. The group average was depressed by the low earnings of the husbandmen and yeomen. As the smallholders disappeared, the group average rose to twice that of workers in 1798. In the first half of the 19th century, as the nominal incomes of the landed classes and the capitalists sagged, the lower middle class and the farmers surged ahead. After 1846, the farmers continued to advance in the age of 'high farming', while the shopkeepers and clerks experienced a fall in income. Their consumption standard, however, was generally comfortable. Farmers tripled their incomes from four to almost twelve baskets over the Industrial Revolution. The shopkeepers and clerks started with five baskets in 1688, reached twelve in 1846, and then dropped back to seven in 1867. This was scarcely above the earnings of a skilled craftsman.

The income of the poor rose gradually during the Industrial Revolution. Between 1688 and 1798, there was very little growth in either their nominal income or their standard of living. In the 18th century, the average poor person got just one subsistence basket per year. The poor did better, however, in the 19th century and by 1867 each poor person got the equivalent of almost two and a half subsistence baskets. It is striking that the real consumption of the average poor person increased by a factor of 2.38 between 1688 and 1867, which almost exactly equals the factor (2.26) by which average consumption increased for the British population as a whole over the same period.

The standard of living of the working class

The working class is saved for last since the question 'Did the standard of living of the working class rise, fall, or stay constant during the Industrial Revolution?' is one of the most debated issues of the period. Everyone agrees real wages rose after 1850, however, what happened between 1800 and 1850 is highly controversial, and what happened earlier is a mystery.

The social tables propose answers to these riddles. Box 5 shows that average earnings per worker grew slowly in the first half of the 18th century and then more rapidly to 1798. This was a period in which there was considerable wage convergence in Britain as wages in the north, which had been lower than those in London and the south generally, advanced to their level. The tide changed, however, between 1800 and 1846, as earnings per worker grew little. The 1840s were a difficult time for workers across Europe, and British workers did not escape the trend. After 1846, however, their fortunes changed, and earnings increased by one-fifth to 1867.

These patterns are reinforced when wages are adjusted for changes in the cost of living and expressed on a per person basis, as in Box 6. This table highlights how much the average household member could consume. One important point to note is how well off English workers were by international standards: The average member of a working class family in England always got more than three subsistence baskets each year, while many Europeans and Asians were lucky to get one. Like the upper classes, English workers did not consume three times the oatmeal shown in Box 6 but instead upgraded their consumption to bacon, beer, and white bread.

While English workers enjoyed a high standard of living at the start of the Industrial Revolution, it was a long time before they realized substantial gains. There was no change in consumption per person between 1688 and 1759, but it then rose from 3.27 to 4.39 baskets in 1798. Stagnation returned in the first half of the 19th century as working class consumption per head edged downward by half a per cent, while consumption over all rose 21 per cent, with the farmers and lower middle class reaping gains of over 50 per cent. In 1688 the average worker's consumption was 67 per cent of the national average. The ratio dropped to 63 per cent in 1759, then to 56 per cent in 1798, and bottomed out at 46 per cent in 1846. The working class began to catch up between 1846 and 1867 by posting a consumption gain of 42 per cent as consumption per head jumped from 4.37 to 6.21 baskets. Growth in working class purchasing power was well above the national average of 17 per cent in this period. Working class consumption rebounded to 56 per cent of the national average in 1867.

Inequality within the working class

If we left the matter here, we would have a view of working class living standards that was neither optimistic nor pessimistic: In the first half of the 19th century, consumption per head in the average worker's household neither rose nor fell noticeably; however, workers on average slipped behind other, better off groups whose earnings rose rapidly. While apparently moderate, this conclusion is still far too Panglossian, for it ignores one of the crucial features of the period: the dramatic increase in wage inequality among workers. Those in the modern, expanding sectors often could do well, while their counterparts in the handicraft sectors did badly. The latter experienced acute poverty. This development is completely obscured in the average. Indeed, the point of averaging is to cancel out the highs and the lows.

We can see the increase in inequality in the Lancashire labour market. Figure 12 plots the real earnings of building labourers, farm labourers, and handloom weavers from 1770 to 1850.

At the outset, the difference in earnings among these groups was small. All of the trades earned just under two baskets, and the building labourers, who received the highest wage, earned only about 40 per cent more than the handloom weavers, who had the lowest. The handloom weavers enjoyed a brief golden age in the first quarter of the 19th century when their income surged to almost four baskets, but their earnings slumped to bare bones subsistence by 1840. At that time, the building labourers were earning three times what the handloom weavers took in. The farm

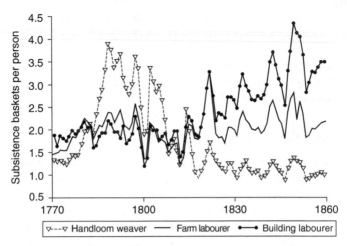

12. **Real wages in Lancashire.**

labourers occupied an intermediate position and realized a small increase in the real wage over the period. The clear winners were the building labourers, whose real earnings doubled by 1850, the farm labourers were also-rans, while the handloom weavers were the big losers.

In 1820, handloom weavers amounted to 10 per cent of the male workforce, so their fate was of considerable consequence in its own right. But they were not alone. Again and again, we encounter the same story: machinery was invented to do the work that a skilled artisan had previously done by hand. People with those skills continued in their trade (it was, after all, what they could do) even as their earnings dropped under the competitive pressure of increasingly efficient machinery. They sank into poverty, and eventually the trade disappeared. Framework knitting and pillow lace weaving are examples.

In 1589 William Lee invented a machine to knit stockings. It was powered by the operator and had more moving parts than the early spinning machines. It was impressively complicated. A narrow frame could make a dozen pairs of stockings per week, while a wide frame could produce that many in a day. In 1844, there were almost 50,000 knitting frames in Great Britain. Many improvements had been made to the frame, which enabled it to knit more and more complicated patterns.

Pillow lace knitting was a separate industry. This was a domestic industry carried out in the knitters' homes and supported many thousands of women.

The industries were originally distinct, but their fates became entangled, as inventors contrived to improve the stocking frame so it could knit lace. It was a difficult problem and was only solved by John Heathcote in 1809. At first, the machine-wrought lace was crude, but over time the process was improved so that finer qualities of lace could be knitted at lower and lower costs. At the beginning of the 19th century, women could make five meshes of plain net per minute on their cushions, and lace cost 100 shillings per square yard. The steam powered machinery of the 1850s could knit 40,000 meshes per minute, and the price of lace had dropped to 6 pence (pre-decimal UK currency) per square yard. In the face of this competition, the incomes of the pillow lace knitters collapsed, and eventually it became pointless for even the poorest woman to compete against the machinery. By 1860, 90 per cent of the lace machines were steam powered. They were operated by men who had formed a trade union and earned high wages. The women who made lace in their cottages were gone.

The fate of the men who knitted stockings was also unfortunate. It was not difficult to learn to operate a knitting frame, so men who had been forced out of other jobs like handloom weaving flowed into the stocking industry, depressing earnings there. By the 1840s, poverty was endemic. The situation only improved when steam factories replaced the old knitting frames. Marc Isambard Brunel patented a steam powered knitting machine in

1816, but it was not successful. Circular machines were developed in the 1830s and became commercially viable after Matthew Townshend invented the latch needle in 1847. William Cotton's first patent was in 1846 and followed by half a dozen others in the next twenty-five years. He opened a factory in 1853 and sold knitted fabrics and knitting machines. Steam powered factories proliferated. Productivity was much higher than in hand work and wages rose.

Modern collective bargaining also developed in the 1860s.

As one activity after another was mechanized, hand workers experienced falling earnings either because their own industry was mechanized, or because another was and workers in it were driven into theirs. Hand workers as a whole suffered falling incomes. The average wage of the working class did not rise until the handicraft sector was replaced by factories.

Education

Income is only one indicator of the standard of living. Education is another. On the eve of the Industrial Revolution, England was a leader in literacy as we saw in Chapter 2. It was common for boys to spend two or three years in the village school to learn reading, writing, and arithmetic, followed by half a dozen years of apprenticeship. This system of education and training was responsible for the widespread mechanical ingenuity that was a bedrock of the Industrial Revolution. Just as the average income of manual workers remained constant through the early Industrial Revolution, so did their average educational attainment: the proportion of people who were literate remained at about 50 per cent.

The problem was that education was in conflict with the needs of manufacturers, who hired boys and girls. Around 1830, the cotton industry employed about 85,000 children.

Many were 'piecers', who tied together broken threads, an essential task. Manufacturers could vote, while workers could not, so the State regarded piecing as more important than schooling, and State financed, universal education was deferred. In addition, the Church of England feared that universal education would promote irreligion; they claimed the right to provide education but did little. The US and British censuses of 1850 and 1851 found that most young people were in school in both countries. However, the American students were all in full time schooling, while half of the English students were in school only on Sundays—their sole day off work. Mr Edward Early, a blanket manufacturer in Witney, stated that 'he superintends every Sunday the education of between 400 and 500 children, and that upwards of 1000 children are taught reading every Sunday in the schools, and writing on Saturday evenings'—after working a full day in the mill!

Not only did the English educational policy hurt British workers by limiting their intellectual development, but it built up economic trouble for the future. The new technologies of the late 19th century required educated labour, and Britain fell behind Germany and the USA, both of which had larger State financed educational systems. The demand for educated labour was growing, but it still took the Third Reform Act in 1884/5, which extended the franchise from 31 per cent to 63 per cent of men, to overcome employer resistance and make schooling a higher priority than piecing.

Health

There was little, if any, evidence of improvement in average health in Britain during the Industrial Revolution. However, there is considerable evidence of growing inequality in health status—as with income.

The most basic indicator of good health is being alive, and this is measured by the expectation of life at birth. Estimates are available every year since 1541, and they show a trendless pattern until about 1850 with fluctuations between 35 and 40 years. Figures like this should not be interpreted to mean that few people lived past 40. On the contrary, many lived to be much older, but the average lifespan was low because about one-quarter of the population died before their 5th birthday. (If half the people died in their first year and the other lived to be 80, then the average lifespan would have been 40 = (0 + 80) / 2.) Since 1850, the expectation of life has risen steadily to present day values exceeding 80 years in rich countries. These gains, however, came after the Industrial Revolution.

Not every group's experience was the same. The family trees compiled by the peerage have allowed their birth and death rates to be reconstructed, and they provide an important contrast. Between 1540 and 1740, the life expectancy of the peers was little different from the national average—in that period, the aristocracy's higher than average consumption of food and housing did not give them extra protection against infectious diseases—but after 1740, their life expectancy increased steadily to 60 years around 1867. What they did to live so long is not so clear.

Other groups were less fortunate. The urban population did particularly badly. In the first half of the 19th century, large towns and cities had a life expectancy in the range of 30 to 33 years, while the average rural dweller lived ten years longer. This difference pre-dated the Industrial Revolution. Cities had always been death traps since human and industrial waste went into cess pits and gutters, while water was taken from wells, streams, and rivers. The wells were contaminated by the cess pools, and waterborne diseases were recycled through the population leading to many deaths. Air quality was poor due to the ubiquitous burning of coal, and that exacerbated respiratory illness. In addition, the overcrowded conditions encouraged the spread of airborne diseases including tuberculosis.

These problems were not overcome until water supply and sewage disposal systems were built, and that did not happen until the late 19th century.

A rising fraction of the population lived in cities during the Industrial Revolution, and that in itself pushed up the overall death rate. The aristocracy in their country houses escaped these conditions, as did the bankers, lawyers, and industrialists who bought country estates.

The workers who lived in cities could not escape, and they paid the price as their young children died.

With urbanization pushing up the death rate, why was average life expectancy constant over the Industrial Revolution? Part of the answer may be the income growth realized by the lower middle class in the first half of the 19th century. They were a large and rapidly expanding group that also lived in cities. Their incomes were higher than those of the workers and grew very rapidly from 1798 to 1846. More money allowed them to buy better food and rent better housing, and those advantages may have helped them fight off infectious disease. In that case, the differences in income translated into differences in life and death.

The study of heights allows us to approach questions of health with different evidence. In Chapter 2, we saw that British workers were the tallest in Europe at the end of the 18th century. They did not maintain their stature during the Industrial Revolution, however: the average height of British workers fell in the first half of the 19th century. This was true of workers in general and, particularly, of those in large cities. This finding is consistent with the rise in mortality that also probably occurred. The height evidence supports a pessimistic interpretation of the Industrial Revolution.

We know less about the height of the middle classes. One sure thing is that they were taller than the lower classes. In the 1870s, the British Association for the Advancement of Science commissioned a study of British heights and weights. Much data was collected, and similar patterns were revealed for men and women, old and young. For instance, the average height of men, 25–30 years old, from the landed and professional classes was 69 inches. Among clerks and shopkeepers, the average was 68 inches, and it fell to 67.5 inches among farm labourers, and then 66.5 among urban artisans. Urban factory workers were the shortest at 65.5 inches.

The upper classes were also heavier. The same progression for 22-year-old men ran from 152.8 lbs for the upper classes, to 145.5 for the urban lower middle class, to 138.6 lbs for the urban artisans. (The farm labourers buck the trend with a weight of 150.6.) How middle class heights changed over time is much less clear.

The 'perennial gale of creative destruction'

It is no surprise that the share of national income going to farmers and landowners declined during the Industrial Revolution, but why did workers fall behind capitalists and why did some workers do so much better than others? There are four approaches to these questions.

The first approach claims it was all bad luck—nature and Napoleon. The wars with France from the French Revolution to Waterloo disrupted trade between Britain and the continent. Bad harvests in Britain drove up grain prices in the UK (cf. the spikes in Chapter 5, Figure 14), and they could not be offset by food imports because of the wars. High food prices cut real wage growth and produced misery. Nothing was fundamentally wrong with British society: the problems were down to ill fortune.

One difficulty with this explanation is that the poverty persisted long after Waterloo. The second approach addresses that question.

This approach attributes poverty to the non-democratic character of the British constitution. Parliament was controlled by the gentry and aristocracy, and they used this power to advance their interests. The Corn Laws were passed in 1815, for instance, to prevent the import of cheap European grain. High food prices were perpetuated artificially in Britain at the expense of workers. Even after the Reform Act of 1832 increased the representation of commercial interests in parliament, it continued to represent the well to do and enacted legislation like the Poor Law Amendment Act of 1834, which reduced income support for the poor to the detriment of workers. In this view, it was undemocratic politics that was responsible for the rising inequality of the Industrial Revolution.

While anti-worker legislation may have played a role in suppressing the standard of living of labourers, the leading social scientists of the period stressed more fundamental features of the society. Malthus' demographic theory is the third approach to explaining the trends in income distribution. Malthus was a favourite of the upper classes, for he laid the blame for widening inequality on the reproductive habits of the workers rather than on failings of the economic and political systems, which might have required their reform or replacement. Malthus postulated that if income exceeded subsistence, as it did in Britain, then birth rates would rise and death rates fall leading to a population explosion that would force wages back to subsistence. Poor relief was no solution to the problem, for giving the poor extra money simply pushed up population growth, which would eventually drive wages down until wages plus poor relief equalled subsistence. No matter how much economic growth there was, real wages would never rise in the long run, and all of the gains to growth would go to landowners.

Malthus' demography was extremely influential. The famous philosopher and economist John Stuart Mill was taught Malthus as a youth, and it led him to direct action: in 1824 at the age of 18, he was arrested for distributing birth control literature to the London poor.

Even though Malthus was endlessly invoked in the 19th century as an argument against social reform, the historical record has not been kind to his theories. While there is evidence in favour of his views from the centuries before his day, the population history of the last two centuries has shown that demography is much more complicated than he imagined. The most common generalization about population since 1850 is that rising incomes have been accompanied by falling birth rates—the exact opposite of Malthus' prediction. His theories are, therefore, not a firm basis for explaining income distribution during the Industrial Revolution.

The fourth approach is that of Karl Marx who offered an alternative theory that also predicted that wages would remain at subsistence despite the growth in the economy. While Malthus explored labour supply, Marx concentrated on labour demand. Marx thought that technological change would continuously throw people out of work. The competition for jobs from this 'reserve army of the unemployed' would keep wages at subsistence. The competitive pressures of a market economy meant that every capitalist had to innovate or be driven out of business as competitors raised their productivity. The twin consequences were (1) continual innovation that raised output per worker; and (2) a static real wage with all of the gains going to capitalists and landowners. These conclusions led Marx to believe that capitalism would be eventually replaced by socialism, which would allow workers finally to gain from economic development.

Marx was wrong about many things, including, in particular, his predictions. Nevertheless, his work also includes valuable insights. Some of those relating to technology have been developed by the Austro-American economist Joseph Schumpeter in his well-known theory of 'Creative Destruction'. Schumpeter emphasized that the important competition that capitalism unleashes is not between similar firms in the same industry producing the same product, but rather from the introduction of radically new processes and modes of production.

> The fundamental impulse that sets and keeps the capitalist engine in motion comes from the new consumers' goods, the new methods of production or transportation, the new markets, the new forms of industrial organization that capitalist enterprise creates...The opening up of new markets, foreign or domestic, and the organizational development from the craft shop and factory to such concerns as U.S. Steel illustrate the same process of industrial mutation...that incessantly revolutionizes the economic structure *from within*, incessantly destroying the old one, incessantly creating a new one. This process of Creative Destruction is the essential fact about capitalism.

The Industrial Revolution illustrates this dynamic. The Industrial Revolution was preceded by the expansion of the cottage mode of production. The first activity to be revolutionized was spinning, as we have seen. Once the cottage sector got large enough—and wages high enough—the incentives for the invention of the factory mode of production fell into place.

This new production system destroyed the cottage mode as it expanded and replaced it. 'Progress entails...[the] destruction of capital values in the strata with which the new commodity or method of production competes.' 'Destruction of capital values' meant not only that outmoded spinning wheels were tossed in the back of the barn, but also that the women with the skills to operate them could no longer earn a living. Their incomes collapsed in the face of machine competition. We saw this in Chapter 2 in the case of the Cotswold villages that had supplied Witney with yarn for weaving blankets. It was a general problem in Britain: the spinners were the first example of mass technological unemployment. The loss of these earnings pushed up poverty in the late 18th century since many families could no longer afford the 'respectability basket' and had to make do with oatmeal and potatoes rather than bread and beef.

It was *déjà vu* all over again with the power loom. The supply of cheap yarn from the new cotton mills led to the expansion of handloom weaving to turn the yarn into cloth. As the sector expanded the earnings of weavers rose, prompting inventors to try to save on the now expensive labour by creating the power loom. Once they succeeded, the handloom weavers were doomed. The power loom was improved throughout the 1830s and 1840s, and relentlessly drove down the price of cloth. Fewer hours of labour were needed to weave a yard by machine than by hand, and costs were cut further by employing women as weavers in place of the men who wove in their cottages. The income of handloom weavers fell accordingly since they were paid for each yard they wove and their productivity did not increase. Poverty grew among the 250,000 handloom weavers, and gradually they were forced into other work where their competition exerted downward pressure on wages. Again poverty accompanied progress.

Technology evolved along the same lines, for the same reasons, and with the same results, in all of the hand trades. A big reason the Industrial Revolution happened in Britain was because it had developed a very large handicraft manufacturing sector in the 17th and early 18th centuries. This led to the high wage economy that prompted the invention of the factory and labour saving machinery in general. The standard of living issue was so heightened and working class living standards lagged for so long because the handicraft sector was so large. Evidently, when any particular trade was mechanized, earnings in that branch dropped, and that decline, in itself, lowered the average wage of workers. Over and beyond that, the displaced workers looked for jobs elsewhere, and their competition put a damper on wages across the economy. The traditional manufacturing sector was not liquidated until the middle of the 19th century, and only then did wages begin to rise generally. One of the virtues of Schumpeter's analysis is that it unites the two faces of the Industrial Revolution: the progress was the 'creative' consequence; the poverty the 'destructive' consequence.

Chapter 5
Reform and democracy

The Industrial Revolution created social tensions and posed practical problems that shaped the politics of the period, and affected much of social and cultural life. Most commentators analysed society in terms of the three class model that was anchored in the economics of Adam Smith. Every price 'resolves itself either immediately or ultimately into the same three parts of rent, labour, and profit'. Consequently,

> the whole annual produce of the labour of every country, taken complexly, must resolve itself into the same three parts, and be parcelled out among different inhabitants of the country, either as the wages of their labour, the profits of their stock, or the rent of their land.

The division of society into three classes is a useful simplification, but it should be remembered that there was heterogeneity of belief and action in all of these groups, and, indeed, their character evolved over the course of the Industrial Revolution. How and when that happened are important historical questions. In any event, enough landowners, businessmen, and employees recognized that they were members of a group that had common economic interests that were opposed to those of the other groups, that the three class model provides insight into the politics of the Industrial Revolution.

Before 1789

Modern factory industries had begun before the French Revolution, but they had scant impact on the economy as a whole. In 1790, employment in cotton textile mills, the principal factories of the day, was only 80,000—less than 2 per cent of the occupied population. Many more workers were self-employed in cottage industries as pillow lace knitters, weavers, and so forth. Agriculture still accounted for one-third of GDP. Although England looked largely pre-industrial, adverse developments were beginning to appear—the cotton mills were rendering most of the female population, who had been employed as hand spinners, unemployed, with a concomitant increase in rural poverty. In addition, the cotton mills were employing disconcertingly large numbers of children whose employment would raise the question of factory regulation in the 19th century.

Eighteenth-century economic life was conducted in a legal framework handed down from the medieval and Elizabethan periods. Statutes like the Assize of Bread and Ale of 1266–7 regulated the marketing of foodstuffs to prevent price gouging and speculation, and empowered Justices of the Peace (JPs) to set prices. The Statute of Artificers of 1562 empowered JPs to fix wages for most trades. The Poor Law of 1601 required parishes to support their poor.

'The principle of our constitution is the representation of property, imperfectly in theory, but efficiently in practice.' In the 18th century, the agricultural rent received by the gentry, aristocracy, and clergy amounted to about one-sixth of the national income, and this group had a higher average income than the capitalists or workers. The distribution of power and authority followed the distribution of property. At the local level, the squire administered the village and expected deference in return. Nationally, parliament represented landowners. The House of

Lords was a predominantly hereditary chamber consisting mainly of great landowners. They also dominated the House of Commons where most constituencies were rural, and many were 'rotten boroughs' with only a few voters whose MPs were effectively appointed by the landlord who owned the village. Parliament was the preeminent organ of government following the civil war in the 17th century and the Glorious Revolution of 1688.

There was a contradiction in the way the landed classes exercised their power. On the one hand, they believed they governed for the whole nation—everyone had 'virtual representation' in parliament even though they could not choose its members—and had a paternalistic responsibility for the well-being of the poor. On the other hand, they did not tolerate royal interference in the management of their affairs, and used their parliamentary power to advance their interests. The assize of bread, the assessment of wages, and the provision of poor relief all proved detrimental to their interests, and they were ignored, repealed, or watered down during the Industrial Revolution. Landowners also advanced their interests through private legislation that authorized the enclosure of open fields, the construction of turnpikes (better roads that charged tolls), and canals, all changes that raised the value of land. These initiatives also benefited manufacturing and commercial interests, as did the State's vigour in protecting property, which included manufacturing establishments whenever they were threatened by riotous mobs.

Most government expenditure was on the army and the Royal Navy, and they were used to expand the British empire and advance British commercial interests abroad. The Navigation Acts meant that the trade of the empire and the markets it provided were reserved for British merchants and manufacturers. While the capitalists were not well represented in parliament, the policies it pursued were broadly in their interests, so there was little to provoke awareness of contradictory interests between capitalists and landowners.

There were conflicts of interest, however, between labourers, on the one hand, and landowners and entrepreneurs, on the other. The disputes were local and sporadic rather than national, mass movements. Conflicts often centred on change (supported by landowners and businessmen) versus the preservation of tradition (supported by workers and small-scale farmers). Popular discontent was expressed in local riots rather than in strikes or mass political movements that were the instruments of the workers once they became urban, factory employees.

Enclosure of the open fields was a great source of dispute. About a fifth of England was enclosed by parliamentary act in the 18th and early 19th centuries. The enclosures were promoted by large landowners hoping to increase the rents from their tenants. While local opinion was consulted, 'the suffrages were not counted but weighed' since it was the acreage each person owned that was tallied for or against. The parliamentary process allowed the large owners to override the objections of small owners. Enclosure often extinguished common grazing rights that had benefited many cottagers.

While they received compensation for the loss of legally defined rights (parliament zealously defended the *legal* rights of small owners as well as large) many traditional practices were ended without compensation. On balance many people lost out from enclosure. They objected to the commissioners and rioted on occasion, but there was no coordinated national opposition that would indicate widespread recognition of common interests.

Food riots were also common in times of scarcity and high prices. These reflected the peculiar conditions of the 18th century—most people were workers or artisans so they bought their food and so they were hurt by high prices rather than gaining from them as cultivators did. There was a long tradition of State regulation to control speculation, mark-ups, and hoarding. In times of dearth, villagers took direct action, often with the tacit support of paternalistic JPs and sheriffs, to find food stored by farmers and dealers, and force its sale on local markets at normal prices. The 'moral economy of the crowd' was in accord with the traditional paternalism. In 1766 the Witney weavers threatened an insurrection unless the farmers lowered the price of corn, which they did.

Machine breaking was another form of direct action in support of traditional practices. The framework knitters, for instance, had an ambivalent attitude towards technical change. Inventions were embraced when they allowed a knitter to produce a more highly valued product like a ribbed stocking, but they were resisted when they threatened employment. Machine breaking could have other objectives as well and has been described as 'collective bargaining by riot'. A wave of machine breaking in Nottingham resulted in The Protection of Stocking Frames Act 1788, which made the destruction of machinery punishable by transportation to Australia. From 1811 to 1816, machine breaking recurred in northern England. The Luddites (named for Ned Ludd who broke machines in 1779) wrecked machinery in Nottingham. In his first speech to the House of Lords, Lord Byron explained attacks on machinery as a response to technical change:

> These machines were to them [the owners] an advantage, inasmuch as they superseded the necessity of employing a number of workmen, who were left in consequence to starve. By the adoption of one species of frame in particular, one man performed the work of many, and the superfluous labourers were thrown out of employment.

Byron's intervention did not prevent passage of The Destruction of Stocking Frames Act 1812, which increased the penalty to death. Machine breaking spread to hand loom weavers in the West Riding and Lancashire, and there can be little doubt that they were threatened by the power looms they were destroying. Machine breaking reemerged when mechanization threatened employment. In the Captain Swing riots in eastern England in 1830, farm labourers destroyed threshing machines that eliminated agricultural jobs. Luddites are often imagined as irrational opponents of progress, but the hand workers were not the ones who would benefit from the invention of power looms even in the long run, so their attempts to destroy them made sense.

French Revolution and Napoleonic wars

While the Industrial Revolution was inexorably undermining the old society, opinion was polarized by the French Revolution, which threw up new challenges that crystallized positions. The French monarchy was overthrown and replaced, briefly, with a democratic republic. The king and thousands of aristocrats were beheaded. Feudalism was abolished. A new religion was declared. The great question was: would Britain go the same way?

The Revolution had many supporters in Britain who believed that democracy would make a better world. Initially, supporters included many who were well to do, but their enthusiasm faded as the Revolution turned murderous.

The Revolution spawned a pamphlet war between supporters and critics. Thomas Paine's *The Rights of Man* was the most widely read pro-Revolutionary tract. Its arguments were not unique, but they were forcefully stated. It made a powerful contribution to a working class point of view, but it was far from the finished product. On the political plane, Paine endorsed the view that people had fundamental natural rights to life and liberty, and that they always retained the right to overthrow a government that did not respect those rights. The Bastille, the prison in Paris where political prisoners were incarcerated, symbolized the despotism of the French monarchy that rendered the Revolution legitimate.

On the economic plane, Paine was equally anti-aristocratic. He believed the land, being a product of nature, ought to belong to everyone rather than a small minority. Land ownership was regarded as the basis of independence in the 18th century. Paine did not, however, advocating breaking up the great estates, but instead he proposed the progressive taxation of land rent to raise money for pensions and social services.

Perhaps a million copies of *The Rights of Man* were sold, and it was read aloud in coffee houses, so many more people heard his words. Universal rights, democracy, and socialization of land rent appealed to many working class, as well as middle class, readers. It responded to a world in which the inequalities originated in agriculture rather than industry and appealed to the weavers and framework knitters as much as to the factory workers. The self-employed artisans gravitated towards a Republican outlook, which denigrated employees as wage-slaves (they had to do as they were told by their boss) and idealized the self-employed artisan as truly free: the latter could choose to celebrate Saint Monday by taking the day off, while the former could not. When the Witney weavers were transformed from independent artisans into factory employees early in the 19th century, John Early, the leading employer, observed that they had 'a dislike to be under restriction as to time'. Richard Osborne, a weaver, added that 'some of them come sauntering in on Monday towards the middle of the day, some get to work on Tuesday, and some do not work the latter end of Saturday'. Workers who skived off were suspended as a punishment. For these workers, the ideal society was an egalitarian democracy of independent craftsmen carrying on their businesses in free markets.

These views had widespread support. The London Corresponding Society, founded in 1792, pressed for democracy and was joined by provincial counterparts. The upper classes were terrified.

If Mr. Paine should be able to rouze up the lower classes, their interference will probably be marked by wild work, and all we now possess, whether in private property or public liberty, will be at the mercy of a lawless and furious rabble.

Paine was charged with 'seditious libel' (criticism of the Crown and government), convicted, and sentenced to death, although he was never apprehended. There was a wide ranging crackdown on dissent. The stamp duty on newspapers was raised progressively from 1.5 to 4 pence between 1789 and 1815 to confine political discussion to the rich. Detention without trial was instituted, and numerous radicals were charged with criminal offences. The Combination Acts of 1799 and 1800 prohibited trade unions and collective bargaining. The old order was defended against all democratic challenges.

1815–32

Napoleon's defeat at Waterloo in 1815 inaugurated two decades of economic and political instability. The next five years were difficult for workers. Demobilizing hundreds of thousands of soldiers and sailors led to a drop in national income and widespread unemployment. As patriotic enthusiasm ebbed and poverty increased, so did demands for parliamentary reform. The result was five years of working class agitation for the vote.

Mass meetings were held to endorse petitions demanding universal suffrage. This looked like incipient revolution to the upper classes. The culmination in 1819 was a pro-reform rally outside of Manchester which attracted up to 60,000 people. The Manchester yeomanry attacked the crowd and killed eleven demonstrators—the Peterloo massacre (see Figure 13).

The government tried to suppress popular protest with the Six Acts including the Seditious Meetings Act that prohibited political gatherings of more than fifty people. Popular agitation for democracy was repressed for a decade.

13. Peterloo massacre.

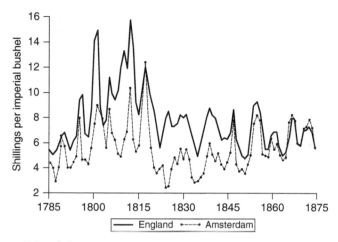

14. **Price of wheat, 1785–1875.**

The working class was not alone in demanding electoral reform. The middle class was provoked by one of the great acts of aristocratic self-interest—the Corn Laws in 1815.

Trade between Britain and the continent was frequently precluded between 1789 and 1815 by war and blockade. Wheat imports were limited. Figure 14 shows the course of prices.

In the 1780s British prices were modestly higher than those abroad but poor harvests (indicated by sharp spikes) drove the British wheat price above that abroad during the French Wars. As David Ricardo's theory of rent explained, high wheat prices caused high rents since rent was the difference between the value of the wheat harvested and the labour and capital costs incurred in its cultivation. The high prices of the war years caused widespread distress, but the gentry and aristocracy did very well, indeed, as their tenant farmers paid ever more for their land. The resumption of peace in 1815 portended a surge in wheat imports that would have driven British prices back down to the

93

continental level. Rents would have dropped in consequence. To forestall those possibilities, Parliament legislated high tariffs on imported corn. In 1814, Francis Place wrote thus to James Mill:

> The legislature will certainly do all in its power to keep up the rent of land, and will pass an Act for that purpose next session in spite of everything which can be done to prevent it. The rich landholders will see nothing but the decrease of rents, and having the power they will certainly prevent it, be the consequences whatever they may.

As Figure 14 shows, the measure worked. British wheat prices remained close to double those in Amsterdam, Europe's great free trade port, for the next three decades. The landed classes did not act like 'virtual representatives' of the whole community, but secured their position at the expense of the workers and capitalists. The Corn Laws convinced many in the middle class that they too needed electoral reform.

Reform was an important issue in the election of 1830. It inaugurated two years of dramatic political twists and turns that culminated in the Reform Bill of 1832. Conservatives aimed to split the middle class reformers from the workers, so that those with property had some representation, while those without did not. 'The real battle is not between Whigs and Tories, Liberals and Illiberals and such gentlemen-like denominations, but between property and no-property—Swing and the law.' Fifty-six tiny 'rotten' boroughs were abolished and another thirty lost one of their two representatives. The freed up seats were allocated to cities that had not been represented in parliament before as well as to rural districts. In addition, the property requirements for voting were lowered in many areas. As a result, the electorate expanded from 400,000 to 650,000 (about one-fifth of the adult males).

Commercial and manufacturing interests acquired more influence in parliament than they had previously enjoyed; however, parliament was still led by rural landowners. And the working class still lacked the vote.

1832–46

By enlarging middle class representation in parliament, the Reform Act changed the political landscape. John Stuart Mill remarked, 'wherever there is an ascendant class, a large portion of the morality of the country emanates from its class interests, and its feelings of class superiority'. The middle class celebrated the entrepreneur, free competition, and reward for achievement. One by one social institutions were remodelled to embody these virtues. In the 18th century, State jobs were filled by patronage appointments. Appointment by merit would produce a more effective, cheaper government. The new ideal was realized at first on a case by case basis and became general policy with the establishment of the Civil Service Commission in 1855 and the first civil service examinations.

Competition would be introduced into religion by disestablishing the Church of England. While this was not achieved, the Church rates that supported it were abolished in 1868 after much campaigning.

One of the earliest and most far reaching reforms was the Poor Law Amendment Act of 1834. England's system of poor relief was based on a series of Elizabethan statutes. Most relief was given in cash or kind directly to the poor—so-called 'outdoor relief'. The alternative was 'indoor relief' in a workhouse. The Workhouse Test Act of 1723 allowed parishes to fulfil their relief obligation by establishing a workhouse. Anyone could admit him- or herself to the workhouse, but the workhouse, often modelled on a prison, was designed to be so unappealing that only the truly destitute would resort to it. Workhouses were unusual in the 18th century.

Poor Law costs were stable until the second half of the 18th century when they began an inexorable rise and with them the property tax that financed them. The causes included population growth, which increased the supply of labour, enclosure, and the amalgamation of farms, which reduced labour demand and eliminated much common grazing, and the mechanization of spinning, which eliminated the part time work of many women. The Poor Law authorities responded to the growing need by providing farm labourers with increased support through such devices as the Speenhamland bread scale, which linked support to the (rising) cost of bread. Malthus gained his renown by arguing that generous poor relief led to population growth, which only exacerbated the poverty problem. By the 19th century, landowners and capitalists alike were convinced that the system of poor relief must be changed.

The machine breaking of the Swing riots highlighted the dangers of rural poverty and prompted the appointment of a Poor Law Commission in 1832. Its recommendations resulted in the Poor Law Amendment Act of 1834 that created the so-called 'New Poor Law'. It stipulated that the able bodied be relieved only in a workhouse. Outdoor relief continued but on a reduced scale. The law also changed the organization of the system by grouping parishes into Poor Law unions that administered the law locally and by establishing a national commission to oversee it. The cost of poor relief fell. The law worked badly, however, in industrial areas since it was not designed as unemployment insurance.

The New Poor Law was condemned by many reformers for its mean spiritedness, and it alienated many in the working class for whom the old Poor Law had been a guarantee against destitution during illness, old age, or a bad economy. The New Poor Law did, however, provide a floor to incomes. The importance of this was shown indirectly when the potato crop failed in Ireland in the mid-1840s leading to the Famine. Ireland had no Poor Law even though it was part of the United Kingdom. Had there been an Irish Poor Law, famine would have been averted.

While Poor Law reform united the middle class and the aristocracy, the two groups were pitted against each other in one of the great battles of the age—the repeal of the Corn Laws. As Figure 14 indicates, the tariff on grain meant that English wheat was twice as expensive as Dutch wheat between 1815 and 1846. High wheat prices meant high farm rents and high incomes for the gentry and aristocracy. Since the standard view was that wages were at bare subsistence, an increase in the price of food meant that workers were paid more money to buy the same food they had before. Rising money wages meant rising manufacturing costs, which reduced the competitiveness of British industry. The gain of the landlords came at the expensive of the capitalists. The commercial and manufacturing classes were firmly opposed to the Corn Laws, while the working class was comparatively indifferent.

The Corn Laws were controversial from their enactment in 1815. Adam Smith had made the case for free trade in 1776, and David Ricardo sharpened the logic with the principle of comparative advantage in 1817. In 1820, a 'merchant's petition' was presented to parliament calling for repeal, but it was rejected. Charles Pelham Villiers, MP, introduced a motion in parliament calling for repeal every year from 1837 to 1845, but all failed. In 1839, the Anti-Corn Law League was formed to campaign against the law. Richard Cobden and John Bright became its most effective spokesmen. The League was an efficient propaganda machine that produced boundless tracts, raised much money, sent speakers round the country, and involved millions in its activities. *The Economist* magazine was founded as part of the effort, and its first editor Walter Bagehot recalled, 'There has never, perhaps, been another time in the history of the world when excited masses of men and women hung on the words of one talking political economy.'

Despite the efforts of middle class MPs like Villiers, Cobden, and Bright, they had no hope of repealing the Corn Laws on their own.

A majority of MPs in the House of Commons were landowners, and they dominated the House of Lords as well. Robert Peel, the conservative prime minister, had opposed repeal for years, but he switched his position and supported it in 1846—ostensibly as a relief measure for the famine in Ireland. He induced the Duke of Wellington to see the bill through the House of Lords as a necessity for maintaining public order. Why Peel changed his mind and why the parliament of landowners went along with him remain scholarly mysteries. Some results are clear, however. First, British wheat prices abruptly aligned with those abroad (Figure 14), but the level did not drop precipitately, and British agriculture remained prosperous until the 'American grain invasion' in the 1870s. Second, the conservative party split, Peel's fraction joined with the Whigs and Radicals to form the Liberals. Third, the conservatives remained out of power for two decades. Repealing the Corn Laws was a great victory for the manufacturing interests.

But the manufacturers did not have it all their own way. They were opposed by workers, the landed classes, and even members of the middle class appalled by the poverty that accompanied progress. One of the first to try to reform the factory system was Robert Owen, himself an owner of the New Lanark mill. In the first quarter of the 19th century, he introduced education for the child workers and replaced the 'truck system', by which mill owners sold their employees overpriced consumer goods, with a form of cooperative shop. Owen endorsed legislation to limit the length of the working day and cut the day to 10 hours at New Lanark. By 1817, he was a professed socialist.

The economic situation for many workers only got worse in the second quarter of the 19th century as the hand trades continued to collapse. Writers of many political views were shocked by the inequality and materialism of these years. In *Signs of the Times* (1829) Thomas Carlyle deplored the widespread poverty, which he attributed to the destruction of hand work by machine production.

> Were we required to characterise this age of ours by any single epithet, we should be tempted to call it...the Mechanical Age...Nothing is now done directly, or by hand; all is by rule and calculated contrivance...the living artisan is driven from his workshop, to make room for a speedier, inanimate one. The shuttle drops from the fingers of the weaver, and falls into iron fingers that ply it faster.

The result was a great increase in the national income—'how much better fed, clothed, lodged and, in all outward respects, accommodated men now are, or might be, by a given quantity of labour, is a grateful reflection which forces itself on every one'—but, in fact, the gains accrued largely to the rich. 'Wealth has more and more increased, and at the same time gathered itself more and more into masses, strangely altering the old relations, and increasing the distance between the rich and the poor.' But the increased wealth was not a blessing even for the rich, for their minds withered as all thought was reconfigured in the image of the machine.

> Men are grown mechanical in head and in heart, as well as in hand. They have lost faith in individual endeavour, and in natural force, of any kind...Their whole efforts, attachments, opinions, turn on mechanism, and are of a mechanical character.

These concerns defined the 'condition of England question', a term coined by Carlyle in 1839, that preoccupied many other writers—among them Benjamin Disraeli, Elizabeth Gaskell, Charles Kingsley, and Charles Dickens.

But it was not simply imaginative writers who exposed social problems. Middle class reformers with a social science disposition did the same. Middle class thinking was usually based on Bentham's 'fundamental axiom, *it is the greatest happiness of the greatest number that is the measure of right and wrong*'. This was conventionally used to defend laissez-faire economics, for if two people voluntarily agreed to an exchange (for instance, a day's labour for 2 shillings) then the satisfaction of both parties must have increased—and with it the total happiness of society—for, otherwise, why would they have agreed? However, if the cumulative effect of many such bargains was to enrich the few and impoverish the many, then there would be a case for the State to redistribute income from the rich to the poor so long as the extra shilling that the poor woman received increased her happiness more than the loss in happiness sustained by the rich person who lost it. Or if household industrial waste draining into a river damaged the health of the people downstream who drank its waters, then again there was a case for State intervention to provide clean water.

Reasoning along these lines led reformers to advocate State action that limited the free market and created space for the State to improve social welfare. Usually the case for reform required facts, and the second quarter of the 19th century witnessed a large increase in fact collection. Some of this was undertaken by the State—the decennial census, for instance, was broadened to track the changing occupational structure of the nation. In 1837 the State took over (from the Church) the responsibility of registering births and deaths. Other facts were collected by special commissions investigating all manner of problems. Non-governmental organizations also collected facts. The Manchester Statistical Society, perhaps the most famous, was founded in 1833 'to assist in promoting the progress of social improvement in the manufacturing population'. Social exposés were the order of the day, Friedrich Engels's *The Condition of the Working Class in England in 1844* being a notable example, but it was not alone.

Working class distress created a political opening for the Tories that did lead to some legislative relief for workers. The issue was the employment of children in factories.

Children were widely employed in the pre-industrial economy, many with their parents and the rest as apprentices or domestic servants. The Arkwright cotton mills, however, employed vast numbers of children who were not under parental supervision. Thousands of children were sent to the mills by Poor Law guardians under apprentice contracts. The State had long regulated apprenticeship, and some ineffectual legislation dealing with cotton mills was passed early in the 19th century to this end.

The first significant employment legislation was the Factory Act of 1833. Its author was Michael Thomas Sadler. He was a Tory MP representing a rotten borough, who believed that the landed classes could govern Britain responsibly. He wrote a book on population that disputed Malthus' theory, he fought to have the Poor Law extended to Ireland, and he opposed parliamentary reform. In 1831, he took over parliament sponsorship of a bill to reduce the working day of children in cotton mills from 12 hours to 9. He chaired a committee that wrote a devastating report on the overwork and abuse of children in factories, and he gave a powerful speech in parliament arguing that employers and workers did not negotiate on equal terms in the labour market—so workers deserved legislative protection. Although his rotten borough was abolished by the Reform Act, and he failed to win a seat in the next election, the persuasiveness of the evidence and logic of his position led to the passage of the act in 1833 that was the first step in reducing the length of the working day. Acts in the next decades cut the length of the working day further and broadened the coverage of the legislation.

Sadler's contribution was also important politically as a step in redefining Toryism. Ironically, the Tories, defenders of tradition, had to constantly reinvent themselves. The political creed of the 18th century—that the landed classes were the natural leaders of society and the advancement of their interests was the first task of government—was increasingly out of synch with social development, so new angles had to be found to argue that rule by the aristocracy was in the general interest. Factory legislation was a new spin on Tory paternalism, and, indeed, Sadler was hailed as the child's defender in the North of England. Red Toryism was born.

David Copperfield and the Factory Act of 1833 were all well and good, but the working class could not rely on the upper classes to protect its interests. What it needed was the vote, and workers mobilized for it just as the middle class had mobilized against the Corn Laws. Workers had been part of the campaign to reform parliament that resulted in the Reform Act of 1832. When they were excluded from the franchise, many workers felt betrayed, and the sense of betrayal was deepened by reforms like the New Poor Law. The working class press agitated for democracy in the 1830s. A group of six MPs and six working class leaders drew up the People's Charter in 1838, and it crystallized their demands. One radical remembered that:

> There were [radical] associations all over the country, but there was a great lack of cohesion. One wanted the ballot, another manhood suffrage and so on.
>
> ...The radicals were without unity of aim and method, and there was but little hope of accomplishing anything. When, however, the People's Charter was drawn up...clearly defining the urgent demands of the working classes, we felt we had a real bond of union; and so transformed our Radical Associations into local Chartist centres.

The six demands of the People's Charter were: (1) universal male suffrage; (2) a secret ballot; (3) no property qualification for being an MP; (4) payment for MPs so workers could serve; (5) equal sized constituencies; and (6) annual elections. Huge public meetings were organized in support of the Charter. It was presented to parliament in 1839 with supporting petitions signed by 1.3 million people, but parliament voted not to consider it.

In response, the 'physical force' chartists turned towards violence. Arms were collected, groups drilled. In 1839 chartists marched on the Westgate Hotel in Newport in the hope of sparking a national insurrection. In a confrontation with soldiers, more than twenty chartists were killed, many were wounded, and the rest fled (see Figure 15).

Armed confrontations occurred for several years, but they were always defeated, and the ringleaders punished.

The core of the protest remained peaceful. Under the leadership of Fergus O'Connor and his newspaper *The Northern Star* more mass meetings were held, the Charter was again sent to parliament in 1842, this time with more than three million signatures, and was again rejected. Hundreds of chartists were arrested and convicted, although the prosecution of the fifty-eight most prominent leaders failed.

15. Detail of the Newport rising.

Peaceful chartists continued to protest and physical force chartists to drill. Some chartists contested elections and Fergus O'Connor was elected to parliament in 1847, the only one to succeed. In 1848, hundreds of thousands of chartists marched on London to present the Charter, signed again by millions, once more to parliament. The State mobilized a vast force to stop them, but there was no violent confrontation. Parliament again rejected the petition. Agitation continued through the 1850s without success.

1846–67

Between 1846 and 1867, the economic situation in Britain fundamentally changed. As Figure 2 and Boxes 5 and 6 showed, the wage stagnation that characterized the first half of the 19th century ended, as average consumption per head in working class families rose by 42 per cent. This was the period in which machine production replaced handicraft methods across the economy. At last, high productivity jobs were being created at a faster rate than low productivity jobs were disappearing. These changes underpinned the rise in wages.

The politics of the period saw further advances of the middle class goals of competition and reward for achievement. Free trade in manufactured goods, for instance, was realized with the abolition of the Navigation Acts in 1849. Working class activism shifted away from chartism to trade union organization. These unions were more concerned with negotiating higher wages and better working conditions than with radical reform. The London Trades Council was established in 1860 and the national Trades Union Congress in 1868. A Royal Commission on Trade Unions in 1867 endorsed them as beneficial to employers and employees, and they were legalized in 1871. Nevertheless, unions did not have enough members to explain the general rise in wages that occurred between 1846 and 1867.

Three events occurred in 1867 that marked the end of the Industrial Revolution. First, Marx published volume 1 of *Capital*, which gave his explanation for why capitalism would never generate rising real wages even though it did lead to economic growth. Marx was born in 1818, and his view of capitalism was formed when he was around 20 years old. At that time the average real wage was flat, and the hand trades were in crisis. He took that to be the norm and developed an explanation that fitted that period. Second, Baxter estimated the national income for 1867, and his figures show that real wages had risen dramatically in the previous two decades. Wages were rising because the old handicraft mode of production had finally been destroyed by the machine mode. Marx was so intent on penning *Capital* that he missed this. Third, one group that had not missed the change was the ruling class. As the real wages of workers rose, they acquired—for the first time—a stake in the system. Their politics shifted from revolution to what would become known as social democracy. It was, therefore, safe to allow them to vote. Disraeli, the first conservative prime minister since Peel, extended the franchise to skilled workers in 1867. The Industrial Revolution was finished.

Chapter 6
The spread of the Industrial Revolution abroad

The Industrial Revolution may have ended for Britain in 1867, but it had only just begun for western Europe and the USA and was still a future prospect for the rest of mankind. Its spread is charted by Figure 16, which shows the shares of world manufacturing output produced in different regions.

These figures are fragile, especially for the early years, but the great industrial revolutions stand out clearly.

In 1750, the biggest manufacturing economies were China and the Indian subcontinent (today's India, Pakistan, and Bangladesh). These were also the most populous countries, and that was no coincidence. Inter-continental trade included few manufactures, so a region's production equalled its consumption. Since per capita income was broadly similar, so was per capita consumption of manufactures. Manufacturing production was, therefore, greatest where population was greatest. For the same reasons, British production of manufactures was less than 2 per cent of the world's total.

The situation changed dramatically due to the Industrial Revolution in Britain. By 1880, Britain's share of world manufacturing reached its peak value of 23 per cent. In contrast,

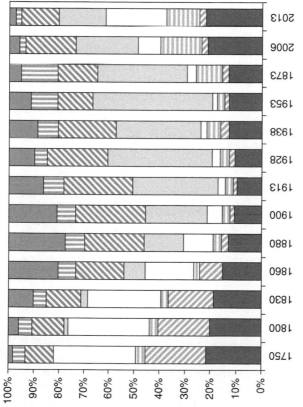
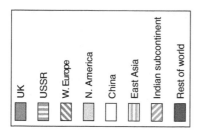

16. Percentage shares of world manufacturing output, 1750–2013.

the Indian and Chinese shares dropped to about 2 per cent each and remained at similarly low values until late in the 20th century. These drops were not just relative but represented absolute de-industrialization as British imports destroyed the indigenous Chinese and Indian manufacturing industries. The growth of manufacturing output in Britain during the Industrial Revolution came at the expense of the manufacturing industries of the 'third world'.

Not all countries experienced this fate. Western Europe's share of world manufacturing increased from 12 per cent in the 18th century to 28 per cent in 1913—a second industrial revolution. Even more dramatic was the rise of North America, principally the USA. From less than 1 per cent of world manufacturing in the 18th century, the North American share reached a peak value of 47 per cent in 1953. This was an even greater industrial revolution than Europe's. The growth of manufacturing output in western Europe and North America reduced Britain's share of the world total substantially.

Two other regions experienced industrial revolutions in the 20th century. One was the countries that comprised the USSR. The Russian Empire had produced 5 per cent of world manufactures in the 18th century, and the Soviet five-year plans pushed the USSR's share of manufacturing up to 15 per cent in the 1980s. With the collapse of communism, the region's manufacturing share crashed to only 3 per cent.

The other region that experienced rapid industrial development in the 20th century was East Asia (Japan, Taiwan, and South Korea). The East Asian share dropped from 4 per cent to 2 per cent in the early 19th century, but then increased to 5 per cent, as Japan built up a modern industrial sector in the first half of the 20th century. The economy of the region was destroyed in the Second World War, but rapid growth resumed first in the 1950s in Japan and later began in Taiwan and South Korea. By 2006, these countries were producing 17 per cent of the world's manufactures.

The final industrial revolution is China's, and it is a very recent phenomenon. In 1953, just after the communist revolution, China's share of manufacturing (2 per cent) was at its all time low. By 1980, it had been pushed up to 5 per cent, and it continued to rise reaching 9 per cent in 2006. Subsequent growth has been very rapid and off a very high base, so China's share hit 25 per cent in 2013. China is now the leading manufacturing economy in the world.

But China is exceptional. Despite much excitement about rapid growth in other countries, their shares of manufacturing output have not advanced. The Indian subcontinent, for instance, produced 2 per cent of the world's manufactures in 1973 and only 3 per cent in 2013. The 'rest of the world', which includes Latin America, Africa, the Middle East, much of eastern Europe, south-east Asia, Australia, and New Zealand, managed to raise its share of world manufacturing from 13 per cent in 1973 to 21 per cent in 2013. This advance is not inconsequential but is not in the same league as the industrial revolutions discussed.

Therefore, the major historical question is: why did some countries have industrial revolutions while others did not?

Globalization and technology: the economics of de-industrialization

The British Industrial Revolution differed from all that came after for two reasons.

First, the British Industrial Revolution was unplanned; indeed, it was unimaginable before it happened. All subsequent industrial revolutions were planned in the sense that countries adopted policies that they hoped would lead to industrial development.

Second, all subsequent industrial revolutions have had to contend with the presence of an industrial power that exported at very low cost the manufactured goods they hoped to produce. Would-be industrializers had to meet that challenge—somehow. Indeed, their situation was even more dire. A country that failed to meet the British challenge did not just stand still—it fell behind; in other words, it was de-industrialized.

The economics are clear in one of the earliest cases of de-industrialization—that of India in the early 19th century.

The British Industrial Revolution took place in a world that was becoming increasingly globalized. The establishment of the sea route from Europe to India cut the real cost of shipping and made it possible for the various East Indies companies to profitably export cotton cloth from India to Europe. English producers tried to imitate these cloths.

Since British wages were much higher than Indian wages, British producers had to invent labour saving machinery to sell anything but the coarsest yarn. The spinning machinery greatly increased British competitiveness in cotton textiles, but it conferred no benefit on producers in India or, indeed, on the continent since their wages were so low that machines did not pay. With machines, it was relatively cheaper to produce cotton cloth in Britain than in India, whereas previously the reverse had been true. The theory of comparative advantage predicts that Britain would increase its export of cotton, while India would import cotton cloth rather than exporting it. Britain, in other words, would industrialize, while India would de-industrialize. That is, of course, what happened.

Comparative advantage arguments are abstract. We can see how the incentives changed by studying the evolution of prices in Britain and India. In the late 18th century, the prices in Britain of both English and Indian cloth were much greater than the price of Indian cloth in India, which is why India exported to Britain. By 1820, however, the prices of both cloths dropped sharply in Britain as technological progress cut British production costs, and the falling price of English and Scottish cloth pulled the Indian price down with it.

By 1820, the English price was lower than the price of Indian cloth in India. The structure of trade reversed as Indian cloth exports ceased, and the country began to import British cloth. The result was the de-industrialization of India. It led William Bentinck, the Governor-General of India, to his famous remark: 'The bones of cotton weavers are bleaching the plains of India'.

India's comparative advantage shifted from manufacturing to agriculture, and this change shows up in the prices of raw cotton. At the beginning of the 19th century, the price was much higher in Liverpool than in Gujarat. The gap declined as shipping costs fell (globalization in action!), and the real price of cotton rose slowly in India. This price rise led to an increase in cultivation and exports. The underlying economics were clear to contemporaries. The British MP John Brocklehurst asserted in 1840 that 'the destruction of weaving in India had already taken place... India is an agricultural rather than a manufacturing country, and the parties formerly employed in manufactures are now absorbed in agriculture'.

The story of cotton manufacturing in India is a microcosm of the history of Asia and Africa in the 19th century. By the 20th century, their manufacturing sectors had been destroyed by competition from factories in Britain and later western Europe and the USA. The economies of Asia and Africa were re-oriented to produce and export agricultural products. When development economists surveyed these regions in the 1960s, they assumed that this economic structure was 'traditional'. It was anything but. 'Underdeveloped countries' in the 20th century were made—not born. They were the products of 19th-century globalization and the industrialization of the West.

Catching up in the 19th century: the standard model in the USA

The first question is why the same fate did not befall western Europe and the USA. The answer is that they followed a set of policies comprising the standard 19th-century model of economic development. The model was developed in the USA since the issue was so pressing for the new Republic. In the colonial period, the USA was effectively in a free trade union with Britain and exported agricultural products and imported manufactures. The USA was de-industrialized from the start. How could it break out?

The first step to an answer was creating a government with enough power to act. In the 1780s the states were united in a loose confederacy with limited powers. The USA constitution that came into force in 1790 was intended to create a national government that was strong enough to develop the country. The constitution itself was the first step in that direction, for it abolished the tariffs that the states had imposed on each other's products, thus creating a large domestic market. In his famous *Report on Manufactures* (1791) Alexander Hamilton, the first treasury secretary, outlined policies that were eventually adopted, including transportation improvements to integrate the domestic market; a national bank to stabilize the currency and insure credit for investment; and a tariff to protect American industries against British competition. These policies were dubbed 'the American system' by US senator Henry Clay, and they form three of the four elements of the standard model.

The final element was mass education. The white population of the USA had been highly educated during the colonial period, and the school system was strengthened in the new republic. The

Common School Movement in the 1830s led to systems of publicly financed schools focused on assimilating the masses of immigrants by preparing them for industrial employment. Together these measures—create a national market by abolishing internal tariffs and building transportation infrastructure, establish a banking system to promote investment, erect tariffs to protect industry from British competition, and institute mass education to prepare the population for a commercial economy—became the standard model of economic development in the 19th century.

The standard model was put into practice soon after the Constitution came into force.

The federal government built roads like the Cumberland road that connected the east coast to the midwest in 1811–16, and New York State built the Erie Canal between the Hudson River and the Great Lakes in 1817–25. The First and then the Second Banks of the United States were chartered in 1796 and 1816. A protective tariff was also erected in that year in response to peace in Europe, the previous decades of warfare having provided American manufacturing with some protection.

While the Bank of the United States was ultimately destroyed by President Andrew Jackson in the 1830s, the other elements of the standard model were repeatedly reaffirmed. Canals, roads, railways, airports, highways, and super highways have always been constructed by governments or with government support. The educational system has been continuously expanded. The USA maintained very high tariffs, which were controversial in the first half of the 19th century, until the 1960s when it was so preeminent in manufacturing that trade liberalization seemed a better way to secure markets than protection.

America industrialized within this policy context. Industrialization was not difficult once the policy parameters were in place. Wages in America were very high, and that meant that British factory technology was the appropriate technology for the USA. Technology transfer was effortless from the start. By the 20th century, the USA became the world's high wage economy and an important generator of technology. What it invented suited its circumstances. It was other countries that had a problem adapting American technology to their circumstances.

The standard model in Europe

The situation was different on the continent. In the early years of the Industrial Revolution, British technology did not pay since labour was cheaper relative to capital in France or Germany, for example, than it was in Britain. Consequently, hand techniques were more cost effective than Britain's factory technology. Western Europe was in danger of going the way of India.

Manufacturing development did not get underway on the continent until after Napoleon's defeat in 1815. Napoleon had prepared the ground, however, by spreading the reforms of the French Revolution across Europe. These included the abolition of serfdom, expropriation of monastic property, a new legal system (the *Code Napoléon*), equality of all citizens before the law, the abolition of internal tariffs, modernization of the tax system, the extension of education, and the promotion of science and learning. The French imposed these changes where they ruled, and other countries like Prussia that were defeated but remained independent adopted variants themselves.

In addition to the legal changes, the commercial prospects of factory spinning and steam power were much brighter than they had been in the 1780s because British engineers had been busy making the machinery more efficient. As modern technology became more productive, it undercut hand methods no matter how cheap the labour had been, and that point was reached in western Europe after Waterloo. In the cotton industry, progress was very rapid. Hand spinning had employed 2,500 workers per 1,000 spindles in the 1760s. Arkwright mills cut that to about ninety workers in the 1780s, and by the 1820s British mills employed sixteen workers per 1,000 spindles. It took time, however, to train a workforce, so newly built French mills in the 1830s were employing more workers than British mills—24 per 1,000 spindles—even when they were using modern machinery. These mills were good enough to undercut women using spinning wheels, but they were not efficient enough to compete against British imports in a free trade environment. It was the same situation in Germany. What to do?

Tariffs were clearly needed but were not enough on their own. The whole standard model was required. It was popularized in Europe by Friedrich List's *The National System of Political Economy* (1841). List was a political refugee in the USA in the late 1820s and was influenced by Alexander Hamilton and the results of his policies. Germany provides a good example of the American system in Europe. Similar policies were pursued in France and elsewhere. The Congress of Vienna left Germany divided into thirty-eight states in 1815. Prussia was the largest and its territories were scattered across Germany. To facilitate trade among its regions, it sponsored the Zollverein (Customs Union) with intervening states in 1815. More states joined in the next decades, and the customs union because the basis of the German Empire in 1871. The Zollverein both created a large domestic market by abolishing tolls within Germany and erected a high tariff wall to keep British goods out while German firms established themselves.

Germany followed the other imperatives as well. The national market was strengthened by transportation investment. The first German railway was built only five years after the first British line, and 63,000 kilometres of track were open by 1913. Between the 1850s and the 1870s giant investment banks were established, and these funnelled capital into industry. Finally, a system of universal education was established. This had been started in the 18th century under Friedrich the Great. Indeed, the American Common School Movement was modelled on the Prussian school system.

Economic development was very rapid in Germany after 1870. A coterie of new industries was created—steel, chemicals, electricity, and automobiles are only the most famous. Many of these had a basis in science, and Germany excelled at them. The German educational system from primary schools through technical high schools and universities was more modern than Britain's, which was held back by its undemocratic constitution. Britain only got universal primary education, for instance, after the franchise was extended to include about 60 per cent of men in the Third Reform Act (1884).

The standard model on the periphery

The standard model was also tried on the periphery but success was mixed. Mexico made half-hearted efforts. In the 1830s a protective tariff was introduced and the proceeds used to fund a small investment bank. The result was thirty-five cotton spinning mills. State tariffs were left in place, so a national market was not created, and education was ignored. The dictatorship of Porfirio Diaz (1877–1911) was more vigorous. The internal tariffs were eliminated and railways built to create a national market. Instead of banks, foreign investment was relied on for capital and to bring advanced technology into the country. Mass education was still ignored. The result was more industrial development based on foreign owned factories and foreign managers with Mexicans doing the menial work. The economic growth that resulted was not rapid enough to tighten the labour market, so real wages stagnated, all the gains from growth went to the rich, and the regime collapsed in the revolution of 1911.

The story was similar in Russia. A large railway network was built between 1870 and the First World War to open up remote parts of the country and connect them to the industrial heartland as well as the principal ports. Investment banks were not a success, so the State provided capital, and foreign investment was relied on as it was in Mexico. The Russians pursued education more vigorously than Mexico had. The result was an expansion of agricultural production and the creation of a heavy industrial sector but one that was not large enough to transform the economy. As in Mexico, the growth that was triggered was insufficient to tighten the labour markets, so real wages lagged. In Russia the revolution came in 1917.

In the Middle East and Asia the application of the standard model was constrained by imperialism. The first attempt to jump start industrialization was the effort of Muhammad Ali, who seized control of Egypt in 1811 and tried to turn it into a modern State. He nationalized the land and divided it into small peasant farms. He created a trade monopoly that bought crops from farmers and resold them in cities and abroad. The farmers were paid little, and the proceeds from exports were used to fund textile mills and munitions factories as well as Muhammad Ali's modern army. Many Egyptians were educated in Europe and at home, but mass education was ignored. The army seized Palestine and Syria from the Ottoman Sultan, who was Muhammad Ali's superior, Egypt being a province of the Ottoman Empire. When the Egyptians defeated the Ottomans and threatened Istanbul, the European powers intervened and forced Muhammad Ali to renounce his claims and reduce his army. In 1838, the British and the Ottoman Sultan signed the Anglo-Turkish Convention, which banned monopolies in the Ottoman Empire, thereby eliminating the fiscal basis of Muhammad Ali's modernization programme. The first experiment in State led industrial development was over.

Nationalists in India would have liked to apply the standard model but could not. Tariffs were kept low and were strictly for revenue purposes. There were no investment banks. A railway network was built in the late 19th century, but it was laid out to deploy troops for pacification and to connect agricultural districts to ports to facilitate farm exports. Building railways was a great missed opportunity. Countries like the USA, Germany, Russia, and Japan used railway building as an opportunity to expand their iron, steel, and engineering industries, but in India all of the locomotives, rolling stock, and rails were imported from Britain. Mass education was also ignored. A factory cotton spinning industry was established in Bombay and jute mills in Calcutta. These industries were important internationally but were too small to transform India as a whole.

Japan would also have liked to adopt the standard model, and its efforts were also stymied by the imperialists. Unlike India, however, Japan remained independent, which gave it more room for manoeuvre. From the 1660s, Japan had almost totally closed itself off from the rest of the world. In the early 19th century, European powers were forcing trade agreements on Asian empires along the lines of the Anglo-Turkish Convention. In the Japanese case, the Americans took the lead when Commodore Perry sailed into Yokohama harbour in 1853 demanding that the country end its isolation and allow foreign trade. The Japanese were too weak militarily to refuse, and efforts were subsequently begun to strengthen the country. The political breakthrough occurred in 1867 when the Emperor Meiji ascended the throne. The Tokugawa shogun, who had effectively ruled the country, surrendered his powers to the emperor, who assumed control. This was not just a dynastic succession but rather a virtual *coup d'état* by modernizers, who set about transforming the country. Most aspects of economic, political, and social life were overhauled.

The Meiji State aimed to force an industrial revolution by adopting the modern technology of the advanced countries. Japan pursued a variant of the standard model. First, a national market was created by abolishing internal tariffs and building a railway system.

Second, a system of universal education was established. Third, a banking system was developed although it was not until the 1920s that investment banks were successfully in operation. In the meantime, the State acted as the venture capitalist. Fourth, in 1866 the imperialist powers forced a trade treaty on Japan that limited import duties to 5 per cent. Tariffs could not be used to promote industry. Instead, the State 'picked winners' and directly subsidized firms it sought to promote. This practice developed into 'targeted industrial policy'. The tariff restrictions expired in 1894 and 1911, at which point the Japanese began using tariffs to promote industrial development as well. Japanese industrialization began with consumer goods like silk and cotton textiles in the 19th century and expanded to steel, automobiles, ships, electrical equipment, and aircraft in the early 20th.

While Japan could use subsidies and later tariffs to promote industrial development, these policy instruments in themselves did not guarantee that advanced technology would be employed. The problem was that Japanese wages were extremely low, so hand methods were often more cost effective than capital-intensive technology. Japan addressed the problem by cleverly redesigning equipment and plant operations to be less capital-intensive. A particularly simple change in the cotton industry was to operate the mills with two 11-hour shifts per day rather than only one as was the norm elsewhere. Capital costs were halved. By 1940, Japan had developed a sufficiently advanced industrial economy that it could imagine defeating the USA and Britain in the Pacific War.

The success of Japan highlights an important prerequisite for successful development, namely, a State with the capacity to set goals and the administrative competence to achieve them. In 1886, for instance, the decision was taken to create a system of universal primary education. This was an ambitious task and took decades to realize.

Administrative and technical competence were apparent before the Meiji restoration, and, indeed, that revolution might not have occurred without them. Thus, Nagasaki was unable to defend itself when HMS *Phaeton* entered the harbour in 1808 to attack the Dutch trading post because the Japanese did not possess iron cannon. The local lord appointed a team of craftsmen and savants, who translated a Dutch book describing an (outmoded) foundry in Leyden and managed to construct a copy. By 1854, they were not only casting cannon but were making replicas of modern, breech-loading Armstrong guns imported from Britain. The Meiji restoration in 1868 presupposed an advanced guard like the lord of Nagasaki committed to the modernization of the country.

Japan may have been unique in this respect. Other countries were held back by political and cultural configurations that inhibited a comparable strategy. In the 19th century, China was beset by imperialist incursions and wracked by the Taiping rebellion that was finally suppressed only by the ascendancy of regional warlords at the expense of the central government. Proposals to strengthen the country by modernizing its institutions were defeated or neutered by conservative groups whose positions were threatened by social change. They had to be swept aside before development could occur, and the overthrow of the Qing Empire in 1912 was a step in that regard. In other countries, cultural features played analogous roles. The vexed question that has obsessed Arab intellectuals since Napoleon's invasion of Egypt in 1798 is the degree to which Islam has promoted or retarded economic development, and, if the latter, how it should be modified to facilitate progress.

Big push industrialization and the development State

In the 20th century the advantages of industrializing became even greater than previously, and, for the same reason, the challenges became more demanding. New technology requires research and development (R&D), and most R&D in the world is performed in a small number of the richest economies. Their efforts are directed to solving problems they face, so new technology is tailored to their circumstances. Over time, their wages have risen and the workforces have become more educated. The rich countries invented technology to take advantage of these characteristics of the workforce. The new technology was ever more capital intensive and raised output per worker. Eventually, the higher productivity translated into higher wages. Once an advanced economy shifted to a higher capital–labour ratio, its R&D efforts were directed to raising it even further. There was, thus, an ascending spiral of progress in which high wages led to new technology that raised output and capital per worker even further and that, in turn, led wages to go up yet again. This process continued until the late 20th century when the spiral unravelled, and real wages stagnated even as technology advanced.

Once the rich countries have moved from a low capital–labour ratio to a higher one, no country (except Japan at the outset) does further R&D to improve the low capital–labour ratio technology. Some modern technology is cost effective even in low wage countries, but not all of it. Some of it turns out to be too capital–intensive, and the lower capital–labour ratios from the past are appropriate.

From this perspective it is no surprise that the one industry in which many poor countries can compete internationally is clothing production. The key technology is the sewing machine. Treadle machines were invented around 1850, and the electric sewing machine in 1889. Nineteenth-century technology was invented when wages were much lower, and it remains the cost minimizing choice in today's poor countries. The advanced technology that poor countries need to achieve high wages and a high standard of living does not pay since their wages and living standards are so low. They are caught in a poverty trap.

To avoid this fate, governments in the 20th century undertook more interventionist policies than simply erecting tariffs. The Soviet Union was an extreme case. Under communism all firms were State owned, and profitability was not a consideration in their operations. Central planners set output targets for the economy and for each firm, and the managers were rewarded for reaching those targets irrespective of cost. When the first five-year plan started in 1928, most of the population was underemployed in agriculture, and there was a great need to build up the capital stock. Central planning proved effective towards that end, and GDP rose rapidly until the 1980s when full employment was achieved. In this period, the USSR's share of world manufacturing rose from 5 per cent to 15 per cent. To continue to grow, it was necessary to close down inefficient factories and transfer workers to higher productivity enterprises. Emphasizing output expansion and ignoring the cost side made this impossible. President Gorbachev abolished the planning apparatus and introduced market arrangements to overcome this problem, but the Soviet Union collapsed before these changes took effect. Manufacturing output has since plummeted. Turning to the 'market' was no guarantee of success.

Latin America followed a less extreme model centred on the 'development State'. The market system was retained, while the State implemented the standard model fully and augmented it with planning and socialized enterprises. Tariffs were high, infra-structure was built, State development banks supplemented private investment, and close to universal education was achieved for the first time.

These initiatives had mixed success. On the one hand, there was considerable growth, urbanization, and expansion of manufacturing capacity. On the other hand, growth was still not fast enough to catch up with the West, and industrial productivity was low. This was due to a fundamental problem: most Latin American markets were too small for firms to realize scale economies. Argentina is a case in point. In the 1960s, the minimum efficient size (MES) of an auto assembly plant was 200,000 units per year, while MES was one million units for engine and transmission plants. Only seven firms in the world—Ford, General Motors, Chrysler, Toyota, Fiat, Renault, and Volkswagen—produced more than one million cars per year. In 1959 Argentina introduced the requirement that 90 per cent of the value of cars sold in the country be made locally. However, at the time, the Argentine market was only 50,000 vehicles per year. Although the market grew to 195,000 in 1965, it was still far too small for Argentine firms to reach MES. As a result, the productivity of automobile production in Argentina was only 40 per cent of that in the leading economies. Scale problems pervaded the manufacturing sector in Latin America, and the low productivity that resulted contributed to the region's poor economic performance.

The poor performance of development States in Latin America, in India after independence in 1947, and elsewhere led many to shift their hopes for development from interventionist States to the 'free market'. This approach was epitomized by the so-called 'Washington consensus' with its trinity of stabilization, liberalization, and privatization.

Macroeconomic stabilization was supposed to increase investment, while the liberalization of trade by abolishing tariffs and quotas and the privatization of State owned firms and agencies were supposed to increase competition. Privatization and liberalization received some support from a related strand of argument that contended that competition between businesses was a source of high productivity since only efficient firms could survive in a competitive environment. State protectionism and trade impediments may reduce efficiency by sheltering inefficient firms from competition. The IMF has been particularly vigorous in restructuring the countries to which it lends along neo-liberal lines. While proponents of neo-liberalism can point to some favourable outcomes—Chile is frequently cited—the Washington consensus has been far from an unqualified success.

An underlying reason that the standard model worked less well after 1950 than it had a century earlier was the evolution of technology. In the middle of the 19th century, an efficient factory was much smaller than it is today. In the 1850s, for instance, an efficient blast furnace produced 5,000 tons per year, while the MES of a rolling mill was 15,000 tons of rails per year. The USA consumed about 800,000 tons of pig iron and 400,000 tons of rails, so there could be many efficient sized mills in the country. Even if consumers suffered from high prices, the high tariff policy did not generate an inefficient industrial structure. The situation in the second half of the 20th century was very different.

After World War II, Japan followed another variant of the development State model that was more successful and turned the country into a great manufacturing nation. Wartime destruction was total. Steel production fell from a peak of 7.7 million tons in 1943 to half a million in 1945 and rebounded to five million in 1950. At the time, MES for a steel mill was one to three million tons, and most Japanese mills were smaller with the result that steel cost 50 per cent more in Japan than in the USA. The Japanese economy was supervised by the Ministry of International Trade and Industry, and it restructured the industry to create larger mills. Japan, thus, reversed the technology policy of the Meiji era when it re-engineered foreign technology to fit Japanese factor prices. Instead, the aim became to install the most advanced technology possible and wait for the factor prices to catch up. By the 1960s the MES of a steel mill reached seven million tons, and Japan built mills of that size on greenfield sites.

Similar choices were made in automobile production, shipbuilding, electronics, and consumer durables.

Who was going to buy all of that production? A large fraction was exported to the USA. Japan benefited from two features of the post-war era. First, the USA was the world's pre-eminent manufacturing nation and felt its interests were better served by opening up foreign markets, so the high tariff policy begun in 1816 was abandoned in favour of trade liberalization. Second, Japan was particularly favoured during the Cold War. The USA regarded Japan as its outpost against communism in East Asia, and that gave Japan more scope for exporting to the USA. The export orientation of Japanese industry meant that it had to compete against highly efficient foreign producers, and those competitive pressures helped boost Japanese productivity. Access to the American market solved the scale problem for Japanese industry and underpinned its spectacular manufacturing boom. The collapse of the Rust Belt in the USA was the flip side of the East Asian Miracle.

The American market was crucial but it was not enough on its own to absorb all of Japan's manufacturing output. The domestic market had to expand as well. The employment practices of Japan's large firms played a big role. Seniority wages, lifetime employment, and company unions meant that Japanese workers earned high wages and could buy the cars and stereos that were not exported. Wages in the fringe of small firms supplying the main enterprises also rose as the labour markets tightened. There was a rapid rise in real wages in Japan between 1950 and 1990 that led to Western style prosperity and validated the technological choices that had been made.

China is in the midst of an industrial revolution right now. After the victory of the communists in the revolution of 1949, a Soviet style central planning system was created. Some basic industries were built up in the 1960s and 1970s—steel production grew from 1 million tons per year in 1950 to 32 million in 1978—but the rate of economic growth was not exceptional, and China's share of world manufacturing only grew from 2 per cent to 5 per cent between 1953 and 1980.

China's rate of economic growth increased in the 1980s, and this is conventionally attributed to the market oriented reforms introduced by Deng Xiaoping in 1978. So far as manufacturing is concerned, the first major reform was the directive to local cadres in the countryside to establish town and village enterprises (TVEs) to produce consumer goods that were sold on free markets. Chinese farmers had traditionally engaged in by-employments, and the TVE was a socialist reactivation of that capability. Since the planners had emphasized the development of heavy industry, there was a great shortage of consumer goods, and TVEs met that demand. Employment in TVEs jumped from twenty-eight to 135 million between 1978 and 1996, and their contribution to GDP rose from 6 per cent to 26 per cent. Market relations were introduced into the heavy industrial sector in the 1980s, when plan procurement targets were frozen, and increases in output were sold on markets. In 1992, the fourteenth Congress of the Communist Party resolved that a socialist market economy was the objective of reform.

With this goal in mind, Chinese industries have been remodelled in a Western manner.

Businesses are organized as corporations rather than ministerial departments. Capital investments are undertaken by the corporations rather than a planning authority, and the investments are financed by banks. There are markets in which products, materials, and labour are bought and sold. Prices vary in response to supply and demand, firms make profits or losses, and firms that cannot succeed go out of business. In some sectors foreign firms compete with Chinese firms.

It looks like capitalism—but is it really? Many of the banks and corporations are State owned, especially in priority sectors where private firms are not permitted. Five-year plans are still being written. The State Planning Commission has been replaced by the National Development and Reform Commission, which still sets targets and supervises firms. In the case of the steel industry, for instance, all of the firms are State owned and all are financed by State owned banks. There is a five-year plan for the industry, which specifies capacity, plant location, mergers, and acquisitions. To avoid having to pay high prices to foreign mining companies that supply much of the ore, the current plan calls for small firms to be eliminated, so that the industry can collude more easily, and the Chinese government is buying shares in the foreign suppliers. Between 2000 and 2013, Chinese steel output grew from 127 million tons (15 per cent of the world total) to 823 million tons (50 per cent of the world total). Almost all of the increase in world production in that period was due to expansion in China. Success was due to planning in a socialist market, not conventional capitalism. Planning, now working through the market, guided the development of other important industries as well—photovoltaics, high speed trains, and so forth.

The economy was directed by planning in other respects. Infrastructure and education (two important areas addressed in the standard model) were under direct State control. Macro-economic variables that influenced the markets were chosen with development objectives in mind. The exchange rate was intentionally undervalued. This both acted like a tariff to protect Chinese firms and an export subsidy to increase the foreign demand for their products. Current planning initiatives are aimed at increasing domestic demand for consumer goods to shift the economy away from exports and increase living standards rapidly.

Comparing China to the USSR is instructive. China has retained the parts of central planning that were effective while jettisoning those that proved counterproductive. Planning investment was the one part of the Soviet system that worked well. Guiding firms with output targets and ignoring costs was arguably productive in the 1930s but became counterproductive by the 1980s. The Chinese reforms have replaced targets and soft budget constraints with market socialism. Much investment is still planned.

Combining competition with planning may have allowed China to escape the contradictions of Soviet communism.

The future of the industrial revolution

Does the industrial revolution have a future? No major country has gotten rich without industrializing. Many countries remain poor, so we must hope they will industrialize too. China is now becoming the source of cheap manufactured goods, and the industrializers of the future will have to compete against it, just as each industrializer in the past has had to compete against its predecessor—the USA against Britain; Japan against the USA; and so forth.

The spread of the industrial revolution from one poor country to the next also affects the rich countries. As a new industrial power emerges, the developed countries have found that they cannot compete against its cheap products either. As a result, the industrial sectors of rich countries have contracted, and their economies have become more service oriented.

Which country will follow China in having the next industrial revolution? Stay tuned as history unfolds...

References

Chapter 1: Then and now

Contribution of industries to overall productivity growth and industry contributions to aggregate total factory productivity (TFP) growth—C.K. Harley, 'Reassessing the Industrial Revolution: A Macro View', in J. Mokyr (ed.), *The British Industrial Revolution: An Economic Perspective*, 2nd edn, Boulder, CO, 1990, p. 200, in conjunction with the average economy-wide growth in TFP over the period 1780–1860 from N.F.R. Crafts, *British Economic Growth During the Industrial Revolution*, Oxford, 1985, p. 81.

Candle making—George Dodd, *Days at the Factories* (1843), 1975, pp. 202–7.

Brother of Lord Chief Justice North—quoted by Keith Thomas, *Religion and the Decline of Magic*, London, p. 547.

Chapter 2: The pre-Industrial Revolution, 1500–1700

Witney's history—Simon Townley (ed.), *The Victoria History of the Counties of England: A History of the County of Oxford*. Vol. XIV: *Witney and its Townships*, 2004.

Cobbett quote—William Cobbett, *Rural Rides*, ed. by Asa Briggs, Everyman's Library, p. 131.

High British wages—Robert C. Allen, *The British Industrial Revolution in Global Perspective*, 2009, pp. 25–56.

Heights—R. Floud, K. Wachter, and A. Gregory, *Height, Health and History: Nutritional Status in the United Kingdom*,

1750–1980, 1990; and F. Cinnirella, 'Optimists or Pessimists?
A Reconsideration of Nutritional Status in Britain', *European
Review of Economic History*, 12 (2008), pp. 325–54.

Chapter 3: Why the Industrial Revolution was British

'Macro inventor' and 'Industrial Enlightenment'—these terms are due
to Joel Mokyr in *The Lever of Riches: Technological Creativity and
Economic Progress*, 1990; and *The Gifts of Athena: Historical
Origins of the Knowledge Economy*, 2002.

Transformative effect of Asian imports—Maxine Berg, *Luxury &
Pleasure in Eighteenth Century Britain*, 2005; and Giorgio Riello,
Cotton: The Fabric that Made the Modern World, 2013.

'Whoever says industrial revolution…'—Eric Hobsbawm, *Industry
and Empire*, 1968, p. 56.

Labour market for spinners—Robert C. Allen, 'The High Wage
Economy and the Industrial Revolution: A Restatement',
Economic History Review, 2015, Vol. 68, No. 1, pp. 1–22.

Share of woollen cloth exported—Phyllis Deane, 'The Output of the
British Woollen Industry in the Eighteenth Century', *Journal of
Economic History*, 1957, Vol. 17, pp. 220, 222, n 45.

'The drawing of one clever designer'—A.P. Wadsworth and J. L. Mann,
The Cotton Trade and Industrial Lancashire, 1931, p. 143.

Britain's share of world cotton production in 1880—Thomas Ellison,
The Cotton Trade of Great Britain, 1886, p. 146.

British expansion at expense of Asian—Stephen Broadberry and
Bishnupriya Gupta, 'Lancashire, India, and Shifting Competitive
Advantage in Cotton Textiles, 1700–1850: The Neglected Role
of Factor Prices', *Economic History Review*, Vol. 62, 2009,
pp. 279–305.

Weavers' wages and invention—Robert C. Allen, 'The Handloom
Weaver and the Power Loom: A Schumpeterian Perspective',
University of Oxford, Discussion Papers in Economic and Social
History, No. 142, 2016.

Christy hat factory—George Dodd, *Days at the Factories* (1843), 1975,
pp. 141, 145, 158.

'Rate of labour is much greater'—James Turner, '"John Bull has a Deal
to Learn" Factories without Machines in the Nineteenth-century
Felt-Hatting Industry', Manchester Polytechnic, Institute of
Advanced Studies, Research Paper No. 39, 1986, p. 9.

Did Newcomen know the science?—L.T.C. Rolt, *Thomas Newcomen: The Prehistory of the Steam Engine*, 1963, pp. 49–57, claimed that Newcomen was innocent of all scientific knowledge. This judgement was reversed in L.T.C. Rolt and J.S. Allen, *The Steam Engine of Thomas Newcomen*, 1997, pp. 37–8. See also H. Floris Cohen, 'Inside Newcomen's Fire Engine, or the Scientific Revolution and the Rise of the Modern World', *History of Technology*, 2004, Vol. 25, pp. 111–32.

'Where there is no water...'—J.T. Desaguliers, *A Course of Experimental Philosophy*, 1744, Vol. II, pp. 464–5.

On collective invention and Cornish engines—Alessandro Nuvolari, 'Collective Invention during the British Industrial Revolution: the Case of the Cornish Pumping Engine', *Cambridge Journal of Economics*, 2004, Vol. 28, pp. 347–63; and Alessandro Nuvolari and Bart Verspagen, '*Lean's Engine Reporter* and the Development of the Cornish Engine: A Reappraisal', *Transactions of the Newcomen Society*, 2007, Vol. 77, pp. 167–89.

'having tryed many experiments'—Robin Hildyard, 'Dwight, John', in H.C.G. Matthew and Brian Harrison (eds), *Oxford Dictionary of National Biography*, 2004. Online edn edited by Lawrence Goldman, January 2008: <http://www.oxforddnb.com/view/article/8338> (accessed 22 August 2012).

Chapter 4: The condition of England

'90% of the lace machines'—*Report addressed to Her Majesty's Principal Secretary of State for the Home Department, upon the expediency of subjecting the lace manufacture to the regulations of the Factory Acts*, command paper 2797, 1861, pp. 29, 31.

US and British censuses of 1850 and 1851—*Compendium of the Seventh Census: Statistical View of the United States*, 1854, p. 148.

'400 and 500 children'—'Reports from Assistant Hand-Loom Weavers' Commissioners. Part V. Report by W.A. Miles, Esq. On the west of England and Wales', *British Parliamentary Papers*. C. 220, 1840, p. 552.

Peers versus national average—Bernard Harris, 'Public Health, Nutrition, and the Decline of Mortality: The McKeown Thesis Revisited', *Social History of Medicine*, Vol. 17, No. 3, 2004, p. 389; Angus Deaton, *The Great Escape: Health, Wealth, and the Origins of Inequality*, Princeton, NJ, 2013, pp. 59–100.

Life expectancy in cities, average—Bernard Harris, 'Public Health, Nutrition, and the Decline of Mortality: The McKeown Thesis Revisited', *Social History of Medicine*, Vol. 17, No. 3, 2004, pp. 394–6.

British heights and weights—Francis Galton, *Final Report of the Anthropometric Committee, Report of the Fifty-Third Meeting of the British Association for the Advancement of Science*, 1883, pp. 284, 292.

Nature and Napoleon—Joel Mokyr and N. Eugene Savin, 'Stagflation in Historical Perspective: The Napoleonic Wars Revisited', *Research in Economic History*, 1976, Vol. I, pp. 198–259.

Schumpeter quotes—Joseph A. Schumpeter, *Capitalism, Socialism, and Democracy*, Taylor & Francis e-library, 2003, pp. 82–3, 96.

Chapter 5: Reform and democracy

'The whole annual produce'—Adam Smith, *An Inquiry into the Nature and Causes of the Wealth of Nations*, ed. by Edwin Cannan, 1937, pp. 50, 52.

'principle of our constitution'—Arthur Young, *The Example of France A Warning to Britain*, London, 4th edn, 1794, p. 106.

'the suffrages were not counted but weighed'—John Lawrence Hammond and Barbara Hammond, *The Village Labourer 1760–1832: A Study in the Government of England before the Reform Bill*, 1919, p. 49.

'Moral economy of the crowd'—from E.P. Thompson, 'The Moral Economy of the English Crowd in the Eighteenth Century', *Past & Present*, No. 50, February 1971, pp. 76–136.

'Collective bargaining by riot'—E.J. Hobsbawm, 'The Machine Breakers', *Past & Present*, No. 1, February 1952, pp. 57–70.

Byron's maiden address—R.C. Dallas, *Recollections of the Life of Lord Byron, from the Year 1808 to the End of 1814*, 1824, p. 207.

'a dislike to be under restriction as to time' and other references to Witney weavers—'Reports from Assistant Hand-Loom Weavers' Commissioners. Part V. Report by W.A. Miles, Esq. On the west of England and Wales', *British Parliamentary Papers*, C. 220, 1840, pp. 547–8.

'If Mr Paine should be able'—Rev. Christopher Wyvill, *Political Papers*, 1794–1802, Vol. V, p. 23.

'The legislature will certainly do all in its power'—Graham Wallas, *The Life of Francis Place, 1771–1854*, 1898, p. 159.

'The real battle'—Lord Henry Cockburn, *Life of Lord Jeffrey: With a Selection from his Correspondence*, 2nd edn, 1852, Vol. II, p. 233.

Expansion of the electorate—John A. Phillips and Charles Wetherell, 'The Great Reform Act of 1832 and the Political Modernization of England', *American Historical Review*, 1995, vol. 100, pp. 411–36.

'Wherever there is an ascendant class'—Richard K.P. Pankhurst, *William Thompson (1775–1833) Britain's Pioneer Socialist, Feminist, and Co-operator*, 1954, p. 131n.

Bagehot's recollection—'Mr Cobden', *The Economist*, Vol. XXIII, No. 1128, 8 April 1865, p. 398.

Quotes from *Signs of the Times*—<http://www.victorianweb.org/authors/carlyle/signs1.html>.

Bentham quote—*A Comment on the Commentaries and a Fragment on Government*, in J.H. Burns and H.L.A. Hart (eds), *The Collected Works of Jeremy Bentham*, 1977, p. 393.

'To assist in promoting the progress of social improvements'—T.S. Ashton, *Economic and Social Investigations in Manchester, 1833–1933. A Centenary History of the Manchester Statistical Society*, 1934, p. 13.

'There were [radical] associations all over the country'—Quoted by Dorothy Thompson, *The Chartists: Popular Politics in the Industrial Revolution*, 1984, p. 60.

Chapter 6: The spread of the Industrial Revolution abroad

'The bones of cotton weavers...'—Karl Marx, *Capital*, 1867, Vol. I, chapter 15, 'Machinery and Modern Industry'.

'the destruction of weaving in India'—UK House of Commons, *Report from the Select Committee on East India Produce*, session 1840 (527), question 3920.

Development economists in the 1960s, see, for instance—W.W. Rostow, *The Stages of Economic Growth: A Non-Communist Manifesto*, 1960.

Workers per spindle: hand technology in the 1760s required one spinner and one carder per spindle plus auxiliary personnel in the putting out business—Robert C. Allen, *The British Industrial Revolution in Global Perspective*, 2009, pp. 185–6.

Arkwright mill—Mary Rose, *The Gregs of Quarry Bank: The Rise and Decline of a Family Firm, 1750–1914*, 1986, pp. 20, 25.

French mill—Andrew Ure, *The cotton manufacture of Great Britain*, London, 1836, Vol. I, p. lxxv.

British mill in 1820—G.H. Wood, 'The Course of Women's Wages during the Nineteenth Century', Appendix A in B.L. Hutchins, *A History of Factory Legislation*, 1903, p. 302.

Arab intellectuals—Albert Hourani, *Arabic Thought in the Liberal Age, 1798–1939*, 1983.

Further reading

Chapter 1: Then and now

A short and exciting introduction to the Industrial Revolution is Eric Hobsbawm, *The Age of Revolution, 1789–1848*, London, 1962.

A multi-authored work by leading historians that surveys much of the recent research on the topic is *The Cambridge Economic History of Modern Britain*. Vol. I: *1760–1870*, ed. by Roderick Floud, Jane Humphries, and Paul Johnson, Cambridge, 2014.

The classical economists defined the themes that still dominate discussion:

Adam Smith, *An Inquiry into the Nature and Causes of the Wealth of Nations* (1776), ed. E. Cannan, New York, 1937.

Thomas R. Malthus, *An Essay on the Principle of Population* (1803), ed. by Patricia James, Cambridge, 1989.

Karl Marx, *Capital* (1867), Vol. 1.

Friedrich Engels, *The Condition of the Working Class in England*, 1844.

A major strand of modern research seeks to reconstruct national income during the Industrial Revolution. Key works include:

Phyllis Deane and W.A. Cole, *British Economic Growth, 1688–1959: Trends and Structure*, 2nd edn, Cambridge, 1969.

Nick Crafts, *British Economic Growth during the Industrial Revolution*, Oxford, 1985.

Knick Harley, 'British Industrialization before 1841: Evidence of Slower Growth during the Industrial Revolution', *Journal of Economic History*, Vol. 42, 1982, pp. 267–89.

Peter Temin, 'Two Views of the British Industrial Revolution', *Journal of Economic History*, 1997, Vol. 57, pp. 63–82.

Stephen Broadberry, Alexander Klein, Bas van Leeuwen, Bruce Campbell, and Mark Overton, *British Economic Growth, 1270–1870*, Cambridge, 2015.

Many historians now situate the Industrial Revolution in the 'great divergence' between Europe and Asia:

Kenneth Pomeranz, *The Great Divergence: China, Europe, and the Making of the Modern World Economy*, Cambridge, MA, 2000.

R. Bin Wong, *China Transformed*, New York, 1997.

James Lee and Wang Feng, *One Quarter of Humanity: Malthusian Mythology and Chinese Realities, 1700–2000*, Cambridge, MA, 1999.

Jack Goldstone, *Why Europe? The Rise of the West in World History 1500–1850*, Amsterdam, 2008.

Angus Maddison, *The World Economy*, London, 2006.

Many older historians still have much to offer in our understanding of the period:

Paul Mantoux, *The Industrial Revolution in the Eighteenth Century: An Outline of the beginnings of the Modern Factory System in England*, trans. by Marjorie Vernon, Rev. edn, London, 1928.

J.L. Hammond and B.B. Hammond, *The Village Labourer, 1760–1832: A Study in the Government of England before the Reform Bill*, London, 1913.

J.L. Hammond and B.B. Hammond, *The Town Labourer, 1760–1832: The New Civilisation*, London, 1917.

Ivy Pinchbeck, *Women Workers and the Industrial Revolution, 1750–1850*, London, 1930.

Alfred P. Wadsworth and Julia de Lacy Mann, *The Cotton Trade and Industrial Lancashire, 1600–1780*, Manchester, 1931.

J.U. Neff, *The Rise of the British Coal Industry*, London, 1932.

Eric Williams, *Capitalism and Slavery*, New York, 1944.

T.S. Ashton, *The Industrial Revolution 1760–1830*, Oxford, 1948.

Other issues that have received considerable attention are slavery, agriculture, demography, international trade, finance, and the constitution:

Robert Brenner, 'Agrarian Class Structure and Economic Development in Pre- Industrial Europe' (1976), in T.H. Aston and C.H.E. Philpin (eds), *The Brenner Debate*, Cambridge, 1985, pp. 10–63.

Joseph E. Inikori, *Africans and the Industrial Revolution in England: A Study in International Trade and Economic Development*, Cambridge, 2002.

E.A. Wrigley and R.S. Schofield, *The Population History of England, 1541–1871*, London, 1981.

Jan Luiten van Zanden, *The Long Road to the Industrial Revolution: The European Economy in a Global Perspective, 1000–1800*, London, 2009.

Larry Neal, *The Rise of Financial Capitalism: International Capital Markets in the Age of Reason*, Cambridge, 1990.

Gregory Clark, Kevin O'Rourke, and Alan M. Taylor, 'The Growing Dependence of Britain on Trade during the Industrial Revolution', *Scandinavian Economic History Review*, 2014, Vol. 62, pp. 109–36.

D.C. North and B.R. Weingast, 'Constitutions and Commitment: Evolution of Institutions Governing Public Choice in Seventeenth Century England', *Journal of Economic History*, 1989, Vol. 49, pp. 803–32.

Dan Bogart and Gary Richardson, 'Property Rights and Parliament in Industrializing Britain', *Journal of Law and Economics*, 2011, Vol. 54, pp. 241–74.

Dan Bogart, 'Did the Glorious Revolution Contribute to the Transport Revolution? Evidence from Investment in Roads and Rivers', *Economic History Review*, 2011, Vol. 64, pp. 1073–112.

Chapter 2: The pre-Industrial Revolution, 1500–1700

Max Weber, *The Protestant Ethic and the Spirit of Capitalism*, 1905.

Sascha O. Becker and Ludger Woessmann, 'Was Weber Wrong? A Human Capital Theory of Protestant Economic History', *Quarterly Journal of Economics*, 2009, Vol. 124, pp. 531–96.

Jan de Vries, *The Industrious Revolution: Consumer Behavior and the Household Economy, 1650 to the Present*, Cambridge, 2008.

Robert C. Allen, 'The Great Divergence in European Wages and Prices from the Middle Ages to the First World War', *Explorations in Economic History*, Vol. 38, October, 2001, pp. 411–47.

Robert C. Allen, 'Poverty and Progress in Early Modern Europe', *Economic History Review*, 2003, Vol. LVI, pp. 403–43.

Francesco Cinnirella, 'Optimists or Pessimists? A Reconsideration of Nutritional Status in Britain, 1740–1865,' *European Review of Economic History*, 2008, Vol. 12, pp. 325–54.

Robert C. Allen, *Enclosure and the Yeoman*, Oxford, 1992.

Jan de Vries and Ad van der Woude, *The First Modern Economy: Success, Failure and Perseverance of the Dutch Economy, 1500-1815*, Cambridge, 1997.

J. Hatcher, *The History of the British Coal Industry*. Vol. I: *Before 1700: Towards the Age of Coal*, Oxford, 1993.

Tine De Moor and Jan Luiten Van Zanden, 'Girl Power: The European Marriage Pattern and Labour Markets in the North Sea Region in the Late Medieval and Early Modern Period', *Economic History Review*, 2010, Vol. 63, pp. 1–33.

Chapter 3: Why the Industrial Revolution was British

The greatly debated question is why the technological breakthroughs of the Industrial Revolution happened when and where they did. The works listed take very different approaches to the answer.

Robert C. Allen, *The British Industrial Revolution in Global Perspective*, Cambridge, 2009.

Joel Mokyr, *The Enlightened Economy: An Economic History of Britain, 1700-1850*, New York, 2010.

Margaret C. Jacob, *Scientific Culture and the Making of the Industrial West*, Oxford, 1997.

Maxine Berg, *Luxury & Pleasure in Eighteenth Century Britain*, Oxford, 2005.

Giorgio Riello, *Cotton: The Fabric that Made the Modern World*, Cambridge, 2013.

Steve Broadberry and Bishu Gupta, 'The Early Modern Great Divergence: Wages, Prices and Economic Development in Europe and Asia, 1500-1800', *The Economic History Review*, 2006, Vol. 59, pp. 2–31.

Eltjo Buringh and Jan Luiten Van Zanden, 'Charting the "Rise of the West": Manuscripts and Printed Books in Europe, A Long-Term Perspective from the Sixth through Eighteenth Centuries', *The Journal of Economic History*, 2009, Vol. 69, pp. 409–45.

Jan Luiten Van Zanden, 'The Skill Premium and the "Great Divergence"', *European Review of Economic History*, 2009, Vol. 13, pp. 121–53.

Morgan Kelly, Joel Mokyr, and Cormac Ó Gráda, 2014, 'Precocious Albion: A New Interpretation of the British Industrial Revolution', *Annual Review of Economics*, 2014, Vol. 6, pp. 363–89.

E.A. Wrigley, *The Path to Sustained Growth: England's Transition from an Organic Economy to an Industrial Economy*, Cambridge, 2016.

Nicholas Crafts, 'Steam as a General Purpose Technology: A Growth Accounting Perspective', *The Economic Journal*, 2004, Vol. 114, No. 495, pp. 338–51.

Nuvolari, Alessandro, 'Collective Invention during the British Industrial Revolution: The Case of the Cornish Pumping Engine', *Cambridge Journal of Economics*, 2004, Vol. 28, pp. 347–63.

Christine MacLeod, *Heroes of Invention: Technology, Liberalism and British Identity, 1750–1914*, Cambridge, 2007.

Chapter 4: The condition of England

Friedrich Engels, *The Condition of the Working Class in England*, 1844.

C.H. Feinstein, 'Pessimism Perpetuated: Real Wages and the Standard of Living in Britain During and After the Industrial Revolution', *Journal of Economic History*, 1998, Vol. 58, pp. 625–58.

Jane Humphries, *Childhood and Child Labour in the British Industrial Revolution*, Cambridge, 2010.

Robert W. Fogel, *The Escape from Hunger and Premature Death, 1700–2100*, Cambridge, 2004.

Angus Deaton, *The Great Escape: Health, Wealth, and the Origins of Inequality*, Princeton, NJ, 2013.

R. Floud, R. Fogel, B. Harris, and S.C. Hong, *The Changing Body: Health, Nutrition, and Human Development in the West since 1700*, Cambridge, 2011.

Bernard Harris, 'Public Health, Nutrition, and the Decline of Mortality: The McKeown Thesis Revisited', *Social History of Medicine*, 2004, Vol. 17, No. 3, pp. 394–6.

David Mitch, 'The Role of Human Capital in the First Industrial Revolution', in Joel Mokyr (ed.), *The British Industrial Revolution: An Economic Perspective*, Boulder, CO, 1993, pp. 267–307.

David Mitch, 'Education and Skill of the British Labour Force', in Roderick Floud and Paul Johnson (eds), *The Cambridge Economic History of Modern Britain*, Cambridge, 2004, Vol. I, 1700–1860, pp. 332–56.

Joseph Schumpeter, *Capitalism, Socialism, and Democracy*, 1942.

Chapter 5: Reform and democracy

Boyd Hilton, *A Mad, Bad, and Dangerous People? England 1783–1846*, Oxford, 2008.

Peter H. Lindert, *Growing Public: Social Spending and Economic Growth since the Eighteenth Century*, Cambridge, 2004, 2 volumes.

Harold James Perkin, *The Origins of Modern English Society*, 2nd edn, London, 2002.

E.P. Thompson, *The Making of the English Working Class*, London, 1963.

Emma Griffin, 'The Making of the Chartists: Popular Politics and Working-class Autobiography in Early Victorian Britain', *English Historical Review*, 2014, Vol. 129, No. 538, pp. 578–605.

Miles Taylor, 'Rethinking the Chartists: Searching for Synthesis in the Historiography of Chartism', *Historical Journal*, 1996, Vol. 39, pp. 479–95.

Dorothy Thompson, *The Chartists: Popular Politics in the Industrial Revolution*, New York, 1984.

C. Schonhardt-Bailey, *From the Corn Laws to Free Trade: Interests, Ideas, and Institutions in Historical Perspective*, Cambridge, MA, 2006.

B. Semmel, *The Rise of Free Trade Imperialism: Classical Political Economy the Empire of Free Trade and Imperialism, 1750–1850*, Cambridge, 2004.

Antonia Fraser, *Perilous Question: The Drama of the Great Reform Bill 1832*, London, 2013.

Peter Mandler, *Aristocratic Government in the Age of Reform: Whigs and Liberals, 1830–1852*, Oxford, 1990.

Bruce Morrison, 'Channeling the "Restless Spirit of Innovation": Elite Concessions and Institutional Change in the British Reform Act of 1832', *World Politics*, 2011, Vol. 63, pp. 678–710.

Chapter 6: The spread of the Industrial Revolution abroad

The arguments in this chapter are developed at greater length in Robert C. Allen, *Global Economic History: A Very Short Introduction*, Oxford, 2011, which also lists many further readings.

The following are a few important works:

James Robinson and Daron Acemoglu, *Why Nations Fail*, London, 2011.

Douglas North, *Institutions, Institutional Change, and Economic Performance*, Cambridge, 1990.

Stephen Broadberry and Kevin O'Rourke, *The Cambridge Economic History of Modern Europe*, Cambridge, 2010.

David S. Landes, *The Unbound Prometheus: Technological Change and Industrial Development in Western Europe from 1750 to the Present*, Cambridge, 1969.

Patrick K. O'Brien and C. Keyder, *Economic Growth in Britain and France, 1780–1914: Two Paths to the Twentieth Century*, London, 1978.

Alexander Gerschenkron, *Economic Backwardness in Historical Perspective*, Cambridge, MA, 1962.

Ha-Joon Chang, *Kicking Away the Ladder: Development Strategy in Historical Perspective*, London, 2002.

Stanley L. Engerman and Kenneth L. Sokoloff, *Economic Development in the Americas since 1500: Endowments and Institutions*, Cambridge, 2012.

Robert C. Allen, *Farm to Factory: A Reinterpretation of the Soviet Industrial Revolution*, Princeton, NJ, 2003.

Ronald Findlay and Kevin O'Rourke, *Power and Plenty: Trade, War, and the World Economy in the Second Millennium*, Princeton, NJ, 2007.

Jeffrey G. Williamson, *Trade and Poverty: When the Third World Fell Behind*, Cambridge, MA, 2011.

Agustín Bénétrix, Kevin O'Rourke, and Jeffrey Williamson, 'The Spread of Manufacturing to the Poor Periphery 1870–2007', *Open Economies Review*, 2015, Vol. 26, pp. 1–37.

Further reading

Publisher's acknowledgements

We are grateful for permission to include the following copyright material in this book.

Extract from Robert Allen, 'Technology', in Roderick Floud, Jane Humphries, and Paul Johnson (eds), *The Cambridge Economic History of Modern Britain*, 2nd edn (Cambridge: Cambridge University Press, 2014), © Cambridge University Press, reprinted with permission.

The publisher and author have made every effort to trace and contact all copyright holders before publication. If notified, the publisher will be pleased to rectify any errors or omissions at the earliest opportunity.

Index

A

agricultural, urban and rural
    populations 19–22
agricultural revolution 3, 6, 24–5
agriculture, capitalist 11, 24
Allen, Robert 33
America, manufacturing 108
Anti-Corn Law League 97
Argentina 122–3
Arkwright, Richard 5, 39, 67, 68
artisans 90
Atlantic economy 3

B

Bagehot, Walter 97
bare bones subsistence
    basket 29–30
baskets, as measures of
    economy 28–32
Bastille prison 89
Baxter, Dudley 61, 105
Bentham, Jeremy 99–100
Bentick, William 111
Black, Dr Joseph 49–50
Booth, Enoch 54
bourgeoisie 62–3, 66, 67
Bright, John 97

Brockelhurst, John 111
Brooks, John 55
Bruegel, Pieter 1
Brunel, Isambard Kingdom 58
Brunel, Marc Isambard 73–4
building labourers 71–2
Byron, Lord 88

C

Calvinism 13
candle-making industry 9–10
Capital (Marx) 105
capital accumulation 9
capitalism 10–11, 24, 80–1
car industry 123
Carlyle, Thomas 98–9
Cartwright, Edmund 5, 41
census data 60, 100
ceramics industry 51–7
Chartist movement 4, 104
children
    employment in mills 101
    infant mortality 76
    as workers 74–5
China 51–2, 55, 57, 106–8, 109,
    120, 125–8
Christy hat factory,
    Bermondsey 43–4

class structure 60–78
  three class model 84
Clay, Henry 112
cloth industry 15–18, 21, 81–2
clothing industry 121
coal power 45, 47–8
coal revolution 25–6
Cobden, Richard 97
Cobett, William 18
colonialism 3, 11, 13, 23, 86
Colquhoun 60, 63
commercial revolution 6–7
Common School Movement 113, 116
communism 122
Cookworthy, William 53
Corn Laws (1815) 4, 79, 93–4
  repeal 97
Cort, Henry 5
cottagers and paupers 64, 66, 69
Cotton, William 74
cotton industry 5, 36–42, 57, 74–5
  employment of children 101
  Europe 115
  India 111
creamware 54
Creative Destruction theory 80–1
Crompton, Samuel 5, 37, 39

D

Darby, Abraham 5
data collection 100
de-industrialization 110–11
democracy 4
demographic revolution 5–6
Deng Xiaoping 126
Desaguliers, John Theophilus 47
development states 121–4
Diaz, Porfirio 116
Disraeli, Benjamin 105
Dwight, John 52, 54

E

Earley, Edward 75
Earley, John 90
earners 64–5
East Asia 118–20
  manufacturing 108–9
East India Company 36
economic change 3, 7–11, 13, 27–32
Economist, The magazine 97
Edison, Thomas 48
education 74–5, 112–13, 116
Egypt 117
electoral reform 102–4
  demands for 91–5
employment and self-employment 90
employment legislation 101
enclosures 87
energy industry 25–6
energy revolution 3
energy sources 44–5, 48
Engels, Friedrich 100
Europe
  manufacturing 108
  northern 18–22
  standard model 114–16

F

factories
  productivity in 124
  replacing hand workers 74
Factory Act (1833) 101
factory production in the cloth industry 42–4
factory reform 98
farm labourers 71–2, 96
farmers 62–3, 66, 67–9, 78
felt production 43–4
feudal system in England 12
financial revolution 7 see also economic change

finishing
    in cloth industry 41
    pottery 55
food riots 87–8
French Revolution 89, 114
Friedrich the Great 116
fuel consumption 49–50
fuel industry 25–6
Fulton, Robert 58

G

Galileo 45
GDP in Britain 8–9
George III, King 13–14
Germany 115–16
globalization 11–12, 19, 110
Glorious Revolution (1688) 12–13

H

Hamilton, Alexander 112, 115
hand workers 74
handicraft sector 3–4
Hargreaves, James 5, 39
hat production 43
health 32, 75–8
Heathcote, John 73
height of adults 32, 77–8
Hobsbawm, Eric 37
House of Commons 86, 98
House of Lords 85–6, 98
Hudson Bay Company 15
Huntsman 5

I

imperialism 3, 11, 13, 23, 86
incomes 64–9, 78–83
    working classes 69–74
India 117–18
    agriculture 111
    colonies in 23
    cotton industry 36–9, 41

manufacturing 106–8, 110–11
    standard of living 31
Industrial Enlightenment 36, 37,
    49, 51–3
Industrial Revolution
    Britain vs. other
        countries 109–12
    British-ness 35–59
    end of 57–9, 105
    pros and cons 2–4, 10
industrial revolutions
    China 125–8
    Europe 114–16
    future 128
    in other countries 106–12, 116–28
    USA 112–14
industrialization 120–1
inequality, in working classes 71–4,
    79
international industrial
    revolutions 106–12, 116–28
international trade 11–12, 22–4, 35
    in ceramics 52
inventions 5, 17–18, 36, 72–3
    steam engine 45–9
iron industry 5
Italy 22

J

Jackson, President Andrew 113
Japan 108–9, 118–20, 124–5
Justices of the Peace (JPs) 85

K

Kay, John 39
kilns 55–6
King, Gregory 60, 61, 64
knitting machines 72–3

L

labour demands 27, 31
lace knitting 73

land ownership 90
landed classes 4, 61–3, 65–7, 78, 86–7, 98
Latin America 122–3
Lee, William 72
liberalization 123
life expectancy 75–7
List, Friedrich 115
literacy levels 32–4, 74
living standards 27–32
locomotives 58
London Corresponding Society 90
London Trades Council 104
lower middle classes 62–3, 66, 67–9
Luddites 88–9
Lunar Society 36

M

machine breaking 88–9, 96
machinery
  in the cotton trade 37–42
  inventions 5, 17–18
  knitting 72–3
  taking over handicraft sector 3–4, 81–2, 98–9
  weaving 41
macro inventors 36
Malthus 6, 79–80, 96, 101
Malthusian stagnation 27
manufacturing industry 6–7
manufacturing, world 106–9
Marx, Karl 10–11, 80–1, 105
Massie 60
Meiji restoration 118–20
Mexico 116–17
middle classes 62
  ascendancy 95
  Corn Laws 97–8
  demand for electoral reform 93
  health 77–8
  lower 62–3, 66, 67–9
  social reformers 99

Middle East 117
Mill, James 94
Mill, John Stuart 79–80, 95
minimum efficient size (MES) 122–3, 124
Minton, Thomas 55
Muhammad Ali 117

N

Napoleon I 91, 114
National System of Political Economy, The (List) 115
Netherlands 21
  standard of living 31
New Lanark mill 98
New Poor Law (1834) 79, 96, 102
Newcomen, Thomas 5, 46–7, 49
Newport rising 103
Northern Star newspaper 103
nutrition 32

O

O'Connor, Fergus 103–4
Osborne, Richard 90
Ottoman Empire 52, 117
Owen, Robert 98

P

Paine, Thomas 89–91
Papin, Denis 46
parliamentary supremacy 12–13
Paul, Lewis 39
paupers 64, 66, 69
Peel, Robert 98
People's Charter (1838) 102–3
Peterloo massacre (1819) 91–2
piecers 75
Pitt, Thomas 53
Place, Francis 94
Poor Law (1601) 62, 64, 85–6

Poor Law Amendment Act
  (1834) 79, 95–6, 102
population change, and real
  wages 27–32
population growth 5–6, 96
populations
  agricultural, urban and
    rural 19–22
  health 32
  literacy 32–4
porcelain 51–2
pottery industry 51–7
poverty 2, 10, 73, 78–9, 98
power loom 82
price regulation 85
printing on pottery 55
privatization 123
productivity 2, 4, 9–10, 124
Protestantism 13
proto-industrial revolution 21
Puritanism 13

Q

Qing Empire 120

R

railways 58
Reform Act (1832) 4, 79, 94–5
Reformation 13
religious change 13–14
rent prices, related to wheat 93–4
Report on Manufactures
  (Hamilton) 112
research and development
  (R&D) 121
respectability basket 28, 29–30
Ricardo, David 93, 97
Rights of Man, The (Paine) 89–90
Roebuck, John 50
Royal Commission on Trade
  Unions 104
Royal Society 36, 47, 53, 54
rural populations 11

life expectancy 76–7
and urban and agricultural
  populations 19–22
Russia 117

S

Sadler, John 55
Sadler, Michael Thomas 101
sanitation 76–7
Savery, Thomas 47, 49
Schumpeter, Joseph 3, 81, 83
Scientific Revolution 13–14,
  35–6, 45
sewing machines 121
ships 58–9
Signs of the Times (Carlyle) 98–9
slavery 12
Smeaton, John 49, 53
Smee and Baxter 60
Smith, Adam 84, 97
social class, and voting rights 4
social tables 60–71
social welfare 100–2
South Korea 108–9
Soviet Union see USSR
Spain 22
spinning jenny 17, 39
spinning machines 37–40
Spode, John 55
Spode, Josiah I 54
spring loom invention 17
stabilization 123
standard model
  Europe 114–16
  periphery 116–28
  USA 112–14
standards of living 66
State intervention for
  reform 100–1
steam engine 5, 26, 43, 45–9
steam power 18, 57–9
steel industry 5, 124, 126–7
subsistence baskets 66–7, 69, 70
subsistence ratio 28

suffrage, universal 91–3, 102–3
superstition 14

T

Taiwan 108–9
taxation 13
technological revolution 5
technology
　20th century 114
　in clothing industry 121
　research and development 121
　see also machinery
Torricelli, Evangelista 45
Toryism 101
town and village enterprises
　(TVEs) 126
Townshend, Matthew 74
Toynbee 3
trade
　in ceramics 52
　international 11–12, 22–4, 35
　effect of wars 78
trade unions 104
Trades Union Congress 104
transportation
　for international trade 22–3
　railways 58
　water 58–9
transportation revolution 5, 7
Trevithick, Richard 58

U

United Nations Human
　Development Index 32
urban populations 27
　and rural and agricultural
　populations 19–22
urban revolution 6
urbanization, life expectancy 76–7
USA 124–5
　industrial revolution 112–14
　wages 44

USSR 122, 127–8
　manufacturing 108
utilitarianism 100

V

Villiers, Charles Pelham 97
von Guerike of Magdebourg 45–6
voting rights for working classes 4

W

wages 10, 121
　real 27–32
Wall, John 55
wars, effect on international
　trade 78
Washington consensus 123
water power 57–8
Waterloo (1815) 91, 114–15
Watt, James 5, 48, 49–50
weavers 15–18, 71–2, 82, 90
weaving 37–8, 40–1
Weber, Max 13
Wedgwood, Josiah 53–5, 57
wheat prices 93–4, 97, 98
Whieldon, Thomas 54
Willow pattern pottery 55–6
witchcraft trials 14
Witney, UK (Witney Blanket
　Company) 15–18, 81–2,
　88, 90
wool industry 43–4
workers
　redundancies due to
　machinery 17–18
　wages 10
workers' conditions 2
Workhouse Test Act (1723) 95
workhouses 95–6
working classes 62–4, 66, 69–71
　demand for suffrage 91–3, 102–3
　education 74–5
　inequality 71–4, 79

Index

working classes (*cont.*)
poor relief 95–7
protests and machine
breaking 87–9
social welfare 100–2
trade union organization 104
Wyatt, John 39

Y

Young, Arthur 17

Z

Zollverein (Customs Union) 115